Sheffield Tr

Past and Present
Richard Buckley

© 2008 Richard Buckley
First Published in the United Kingdom, 2008
Stenlake Publishing Limited
54-58 Mill Square, Catrine, KA5 6RD
01290 551122
www.stenlake.co.uk

ISBN 9781840334364

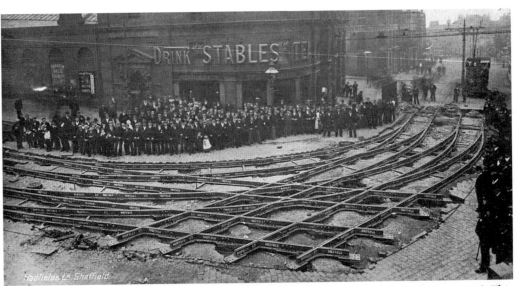

In Bristol over half the tram routes ended at or passed by a central terminus known as the Tramways Centre and five more routes did so at Old Market. In a similar move, in 1900, about a year after electric tram services began in Sheffield, a proposal was made to construct an elaborate turning and reversing facility in or near Fitzalan Square, but in the end it was decided to run most trams on cross-city services. Nevertheless a number of routes always did end or pass here, many more if the street across the far end is counted. This photograph of tracklaying is from an Edwardian catalogue for Hadfield's Steel Foundry Co. Ltd., a Sheffield firm. The son of the founder, Sir Robert Hadfield, was an analytical chemist who, in 1882, discovered manganese steel, an alloy with the remarkable property of hardening with use. It could be used either for complete tramway points and crossings or, more economically, as inserts in cast steel work. The catalogue says that though this junction was 'the key to the whole system it was originally a continual source of trouble and expense... it was relaid by Hadfields entirely in Era Manganese Steel in September, 1901, and up to June, 1906, the total number of cars that passed over it amounted to something like 4 ½ millions'.

Acknowledgements

I am grateful to all who have assisted me with fresh and corrected details of the two Sheffield tramway systems, particularly Paul Jackson and Pat Malham who commented on the first draft in helpful detail. Roger Smith drew the two maps to his usual high standard. Glynn Wilton at the National Tramway Museum gave useful advice on copyright matters and also granted permission to reproduce two pictures by M. J. O'Connor and one by H. B. Priestley. Collected cuttings from the (Sheffield) Star and Telegraph have jogged my memory and, not least, provided human interest stories to add to the bald facts.

Several views can be found on the web site www.picturesheffield.com. Some old postcards came from the collections of Geoff Smith and Mel Jones. A few photographs are by or from the collection of David Packer. My main debt is to Richard Wiseman who has generously allowed me to choose from the immense archive of his own photographs dating from 1947-1960 as well as from his collection of postcards etc. The cover pictures were taken by him. I am grateful to all those named. Many of the earlier pictures are taken from commercial postcards. So far as any later views not acknowledged above go, a number (including all the Supertram ones) are my own and, for the rest, it has not been possible to trace a copyright owner. I trust any who read this will forgive the omission.

Further Reading

Bett W. H. & Gillham J. C., *The Tramways of South Yorkshire and Humberside*, ed. Price, J. H., 1975

Battersby P., *Super Prestige: Sheffield*

Fox, P., Jackson P. & Benton R., *Tram to Supertram*, 1995

Gandy K., *Sheffield Corporation Tramways*, 1985

Hall, C. C., *Sheffield Transport*, 1977

Hey D., *A History of Sheffield*, 2005

Mettam B., *Riding the Sheffield Lines*, 2006

Sheffield Transport Department, *Sheffield Municipal Transport 1896-1946*, 1946

Sheffield Transport Department, *The Tramway Era in Sheffield*, 1960

Twidale, G. H. E., *A nostalgic look at Sheffield Trams since 1950*, 1995

Wiseman R. J. S., *British Tramways in Pictures 1. Sheffield.* 1964

www.picturesheffield.com is the Sheffield Archives site with an invaluable online collection of predominantly nineteenth and early twentieth century Sheffield photographs

Introduction

Sheffield people have a wry sense of humour and like to remark that their city is built upon seven hills like Rome. Actually there are good many more than that and, except for the Don Valley towards Rotherham, flat land is at a premium. It was the rivers running down these hills, the Don, Loxley, Porter, Rivelin and Sheaf, that determined the town's development into an industrial centre as these provided the necessary power for iron foundries, forging hammers and grinding wheels. There is plentiful coal and gritstone in the area, but apart from that, natural resources were surprisingly sparse. The local iron ore was soon outgrown, as was the reliance upon charcoal from the woods and coppices. Sheffield initially became known for its knives, cutlery and edge tools in general. It was only from the mid-eighteenth Century that large-scale steel manufacture first rivalled and then eventually almost entirely overtook the older trades. Sheffield Plate was an once-important local invention and silverware is still designed and made today.

Local government was largely in the hands of the magistracy until quite late. Sheffield did not become a borough until 1843 and a city fifty years after that. By 1911 its population exceeded that of Leeds, making it the fifth city in England.

Manufacturing trade could not have developed without transport. Throughout the Middle Ages most goods were carried by packhorse as Sheffield had no access to a navigable waterway, a deficiency remedied in 1751 when the Don Navigation was completed as far as Tinsley. Eventually a flight of locks was built there with a canal right to the centre

of the city which opened in 1819. The first toll road was authorised in 1756 along The Moor and through Heeley towards Derby and, ultimately, London; coach services were eventually provided to many destinations. Railways were more difficult due to the surrounding hills. George Stephenson's North Midland Railway was opened in 1840 but only to a station at Rotherham, though a connecting line from Sheffield already existed. The Woodhead route from Manchester was completed by 1851 and it was possible to catch a through train from its new Victoria Station to London via Retford from the mid-1850s. The direct Midland line from Derby via the Bradway tunnel was, however, greeted with considerable excitement when it opened on 1 February 1870 to what is now Sheffield Station. By this date there were also about a dozen suburban stations in addition to the two main termini.

The first local public road transport was provided from 1852 by horse buses. The Sheffield Tramways Company secured powers to construct a nine mile horse-powered system in 1872 and the Corporation used the option of building and leasing back the tracks, as was permitted under the 1870 Tramways Act. The first line opened in 1873. Up to four experiments were made with steam tram engines but nothing came of them. In 1896 Sheffield Corporation bought the company's assets and by the following year had decided upon conversion to an overhead electrical system. However, it was still necessary to buy some more horse cars and to work certain new routes with them as a temporary measure and as a result horse trams ran until 11 November 1902 and the final horse route was not fully reconstructed until 30 May 1903. The first electric trams started on 5 September 1899. The system expanded rapidly thereafter and by 1914 there were fourteen routes. A through service was also run jointly with Rotherham Corporation. Motorbuses were first used in 1913-14. After the Great War tramway expansion was resumed until the last line was opened on 29 December 1935. However, there were also three route closures, Petre Street in 1925, Nether Edge in 1934 and Fulwood via Broomhill in 1936. With the exception of fifteen trams the entire fleet was renewed between 1918 and 1939. The addition of some wartime replacement trams meant that the fleet reached its maximum size of 468 at the end of 1944 and in 1945-1946 there were 199 million passengers.

Following World War Two a further thirty-six cars of strikingly modern appearance were delivered. At the same time, however, both costs and

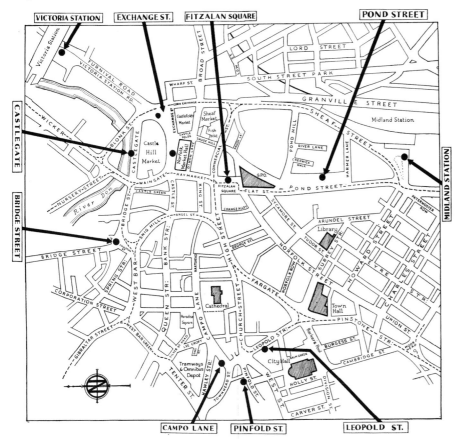

road traffic were rising sharply and official opinion was that buses would be cheaper, easier to integrate with road improvements and also safer for passengers. The public did not agree! However, in 1951 the City Council accepted a report recommending the withdrawal of trams and, as was usual in such cases, this was achieved more quickly than originally planned. What was confidently expected to be Sheffield's Last Tram ran on 8 October 1960, just a handful being saved for preservation, most of them by the embryonic Tramway Museum Society.

However, as early as 1971-1975 a study recommended protecting certain possible alignments for rapid transit and ten years later parliamentary powers were sought for what became the Halfway – Middlewood/Malin Bridge Supertram line. Meanwhile the City Council had proposed a second line to serve the Lower Don Valley. Acts of Parliament were passed in 1988 and 1989 for these and the following year funding was agreed. A Design & Build contract was let to Balfour Beatty and work was well under way by Spring 1992. Points and crossings were supplied by the local track specialists, Edgar Allen Engineering, and the trams were built in Germany by Siemens at their recently acquired Düwag factory in Düsseldorf. Test runs began in September 1993 and public service from Fitzalan Square to Meadowhall followed on 21 March 1994.

The remainder of the system then opened in stages and was completed with the Middlewood line and the Malin Bridge branch on 23 October 1995. The publicly-owned operator was making considerable and disappointing losses but, in any case, privatisation had always been foreseen. In 1997 the cars and infrastructure were sold to a banking consortium and the operating rights to the major bus operator, Stagecoach. The South Yorkshire Passenger Transport Executive (PTE) retains a regulatory role. Stagecoach introduced various immediate improvements and within a few years could report greatly increased traffic and an operating profit. Sadly in July 2006 the Government turned down the Passenger Transport Authority's request for funding for two extensions, one to Rotherham and the other a short loop to serve the Hallamshire Hospital in Sheffield, but otherwise the system remains in good heart and it is difficult to imagine Sheffield without it.

The Corporation tram lines were officially regarded as sections, usually from city centre to suburb. Most were operated as cross-city lines though not necessarily using identical pairings or to the same terminus. Previous arrangements are noted where appropriate, but the municipal tramways are treated here as they were from the 1940s until closure. The routes are described and illustrated by section, usually working from the city centre out to the suburb concerned. First of all the northern lines are dealt with and then the rest, clock-face style. Supertram is fitted into this scheme. Reference should be made throughout to the two maps.

This postcard view, sent in October 1904, shows the terminal siding in Fitzalan Square. The centre of the square was at that time occupied by an edifice known either as the (horse) omnibus waiting room or the cabmen's shelter. There are certainly plenty of Hansom cabs lined up waiting for fares. The low building in the left background is the Fitzalan Market, a predecessor to both the Norfolk and Castle Markets. On the right Wonderland is described as an entertainment booth. Car 47, built by George F. Milnes & Co, Birkenhead, is one of the very first trams delivered in 1899 and is in its original open-fronted condition. The similar car 46 is preserved at the National Tramway Museum at Crich in Derbyshire.

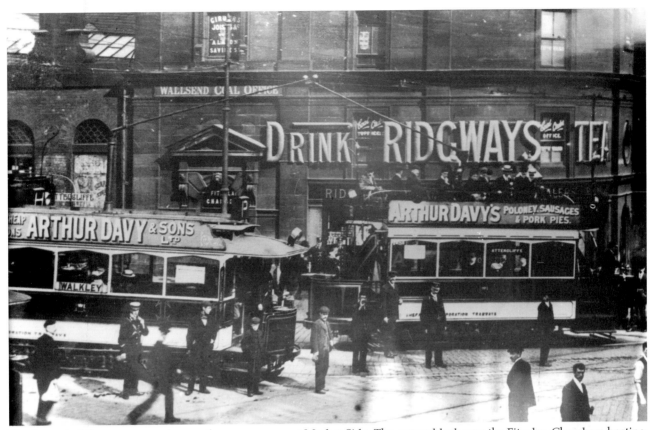

The far end of the square was known for many years as Market Side. The corner block was the Fitzalan Chambers hosting, variously, a coal office and a well-advertised Ridgeway's Tea Shop. Two types of tram were purchased to inaugurate electric services in 1899 and both are shown negotiating the curve at the corner with Haymarket. The smaller car displays route letter P for Pitsmoor but is going to Walkley, demonstrating the obvious deficiency of using letters as route indicators. The destination of the other tram is Attercliffe and it already seems to have a route blind in the side window, making the date around 1905-10, when the newer system was introduced. A little earlier, in 1902, the tramways' department had introduced posting boxes on late evening trams. The tin boxes were presumably taken off here for the GPO, which was just off Fitzalan Square. The collection was a war casualty in 1939.

This time the photographer is standing on the pavement in front of the market hall. The extravagant decorations are for the visit of Edward VII and Queen Alexandra on 12 June 1905 to open the new Sheffield University. The car has come from Millhouses and, after passing the two impressive lions rampant, will turn left into Haymarket en route to Tinsley. This was one of the lines which opened on the first day of operation, 5 September 1899.

This nice view is of the top of Haymarket after World War Two. Bomb damage is visible to the left but the horse-drawn dray had still not quite disappeared from the streets. The overhead linesmen's skill is well displayed here. The large building to the right behind the trams is the old Norfolk Market Hall, erected in 1851 when the 13th Duke of Norfolk still held the market rights in the city; it was demolished in 1959 to make way for shops and for the new municipal Castle Markets, built opposite. That was also the year in which the Yorkshire Bank dropped the Penny from its title.

Rather strangely, the royal visit in mid-summer 1905 seems to have been marked by rows of Christmas trees along Lady's Bridge! The wood and plasterboard triumphal arch includes the Latin phrase 'Iam Fides et Pax et Honor', 'Henceforth faith, peace and honour'. King Edward was known as the Peacemaker due to his good relations with most European states and leaders, especially the French, though sadly this didn't include his nephew, Kaiser Wilhelm of Germany. They famously disliked each other! To the left the overhead wiring leads into Bridge Street. The building with the stepped gable to the right was built for the Midland Railway in the mid-1900s and still stands. Car 16, approaching down the Wicker, was an 1899 Milnes car.

The only other purpose-built central terminus was Exchange Street, opened on 22 September 1924. The loop, seen here before the Brightside & Carbrook Co-operative store was bombed in 1940, was used by the Sheffield to Rotherham service. Rotherham 2 was one of eleven new English Electric Co. trams bought in 1934-1935 to maintain what was to become their only remaining tram service. All other routes were withdrawn in 1933-39. (R.J.S.Wiseman's coll.)

Having crossed the river, all the northern routes used the Wicker, originally an open space beneath the medieval castle intended for archery practice and feudal assemblies, at the end of which are the impressive Wicker Arches. In 1954 the railway to Manchester via Woodhead pioneered main line electrification in the UK at 1500 volts d.c. power supply. All that remains today is a diesel-worked freight line to the steel works at Stocksbridge. Beyond the bridge is Savile Street and this really marks the transition between the city centre and the East End. There was a stairway and a lift up to Victoria Station in the building to the right of the second tram. The viaduct had brought the Manchester, Sheffield & Lincolnshire Railway to Sheffield's first main line station here in 1851. The terminus was described at the time as 'covered with a light glass roof like that of the Crystal Palace' though Pevsner, a century on, thought it a gloomy entry into Sheffield. All the more so on a cold February day in 1954. (R. J. S. Wiseman)

After leaving the Wicker, the tracks for Tinsley briefly touched Savile Street before joining Attercliffe Road where 175 is shown returning to City (never 'City Centre' in Sheffield). It might be on a Handsworth or Prince of Wales Road working rather than Tinsley. This is Norfolk Bridge carrying the former Midland Railway line. There is a lengthy viaduct either side of it and perched on it nearby was the former Attercliffe Road Station, one of two in Sheffield offering only passenger facilities. It was closed as redundant once Supertram opened. The primitive corrugated iron shelter on the far side was for outward bound tram passengers. (R.J.S.Wiseman)

Around 1905 the electric tram was the king of the road! Virtually every other vehicle, such as the dustcart drawn up alongside the pavement and the passing butcher's cart, was horse-drawn. This is Attercliffe, which was then a teeming working class community. The Council's housing clearances – after the tramways had closed – reduced the population in the Lower Don Valley from about ten thousand down to less than two hundred. 142 was one of a second series of Milnes trams. Advertisements along the top deck sides were carried in the period 1903-1916. Some other views show the intricate lining out originally applied to these cars prior to that. All the open-toppers were roofed like this in 1903-1910, retaining their original equipment. 246-257 were built new by SCT at the Nether Edge works in 1905. For its period this was a very handsome design giving a light and airy covered top deck. Many cars were further rebuilt, several were sold and five converted into works cars, including 142 which became snowplough 371. (picturesheffield.com)

At the end of the 1950s there were still rows and rows of terrace housing in Attercliffe and Tinsley. Nowadays builders merchants or DIY warehouses have taken over the trade of small ironmongers like the one behind the lorry. The lorry is one of a fleet running a regular service to Hull along what was the main road to Rotherham as well as being a residential street. Car 504 is on the through tram route to Vulcan Road.

This photograph was taken at the Tinsley terminus on Attercliffe Common. The first electric trams in Sheffield started in 1899 between this point and Nether Edge although, as the letter M shows, the second destination was soon switched to Millhouses. The only other route indication in the early 1900s was provided by a board on the side of the car. This shot gives a good impression of what the highly successful 21E truck looked like. This was to the design of the J.G.Brill Co, Philadelphia, USA, later licensed for UK manufacture. Pedestrian safety was assured by the lifeguards on each end. The idea – broadly borne out in practice – was that the trays would scoop up anyone unfortunate enough to fall under the tram. (picturesheffield.com)

This is Weedon Street just beyond the 1899 terminus. A line down here may have existed to take horse trams from the company's works at Tinsley to Brightside Depot but this remains to be confirmed. An electric extension was partially built in 1902-3 but never completed. Only the siding at the Tinsley end came into use as a new terminus. The Commercial Hotel, just behind the tram, meant that the entrance to the depot itself was always very restricted. There was a double track in the 'to city' direction and a single trailing connection from the depot, just visible beneath the car. Quite a few years ago Weedon Street became a busy road link to Brightside, but in 2008 the depot still stood beside it. It is protected by listed status but is only partially occupied and in poor repair. 287 is one of the immediately pre-war trams, usually known as domed-roof cars. When new the roof was painted cream but that was replaced by dark grey as a wartime precaution against air raids.

The company's initial horse line opened as far as Attercliffe on 6 October 1873 and to Tinsley (described as Carbrook) on 7 May 1874. Car 10 has probably been pushed out of the depot there for the photographer. Even if there were no horses available it would have been an easy task for two or three men as horse trams were quite light. The staircases here look dangerously flimsy. Later photographs show that both the stairs and upper deck rails were panelled in with so-called decency boards. The two-horse cars numbers 1-12, with longitudinal seating on both decks, were delivered for the

opening by the Starbuck Car & Wagon Co., Birkenhead, quite a well known builder of tram cars in the pre-electric period. Seating was longitudinal on both decks. The bench along the centre of the roof line on top was known as a knifeboard, a term taken from a board on which knives were cleaned. The city terminus for both the Attercliffe and Brightside horse routes was Lady's Bridge. (R.J.S.Wiseman's coll)

TINSLEY DEPOT
C. 1898

The depot was one of the original Tramway Company buildings and was first used as a stable from 6 October 1873 and then as a depot from 7 May the following year. In the interim the cars were kept at temporary premises on Newhall Road. In 1898 work was well under way to convert it to a Corporation electric depot with a larger shed, new rails and overhead poles and wires. Where the horses and their cars were kept in the meantime is not known, but they seem to have kept running until electric services began. The new section replaced the old stables, which were demolished. Part of the building was used as a body shop until a fire in 1910. The power was finally turned off on 8 October 1960, though disused trams were stored there for several months longer awaiting space at the scrapyard.

This is the yard outside Tinsley Depot and the view must have been taken prior to 1952/3 as the passenger tram is not carrying advertisements as was usual after this, but instead has the Sheffield Transport Department monogram on the top deck as it had when new. The preceding car has been specially decorated for a Road Courtesy Week. It is believed to be based on the truck of balcony car 353, first used for a similar purpose for George V's Silver Jubilee in 1935. Car 353 was renumbered 310 after 1945 and scrapped in 1953.

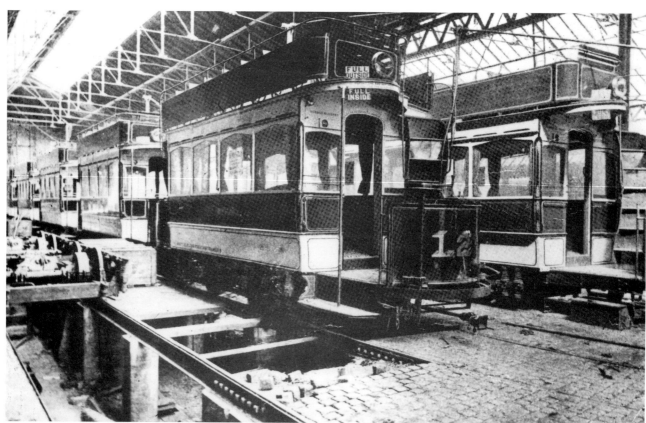

One hundred and seventy-two open-top cars were purchased in 1899-1904. All had wooden longitudinal seats below and transverse above. Car 12 is seen in a line of similar cars in Tinsley Depot before services began. The 'full inside and outside' signs never appear to have been used and the curtains would soon have been removed as redundant. All cars were later top covered. Sixty years later 1936-type 297 is being driven through the narrow entrance to the depot yard in the summer of 1959. It was certainly withdrawn that year perhaps a month or so after this. However, given the damage it has sustained in a collision, this might have been its last trip under power. If so, it would have been stored on some of the spare tracks inside the sheds until there was space for it at the nearby scrapyard.

The depot was closed as a running shed on 3 October 1959 but even after that when a tram was withdrawn it was driven to Tinsley and kept there until there was space in the scrapyard. T.W.Ward's yard was just across the road and each tram was shunted across using a lorry. This works car is making its final journey in April 1960, a few months before the running line itself would see its last tram. 365 was a snowplough adapted from the 1900 double decker 77 and had the characteristic flat roof of such a conversion. It may not have been used during the winter of 1959-60 and it was evidently reluctant to move this time, but plenty of onlookers were ready with advice. Overhead poles also ended up at Ward's but not usually the track. Very often this was simply buried under a new road surface. As late as 2007 major roadworks on the Wicker for the new section of the ring road revealed a lot of rail which was only then torn up, nearly fifty years after it had last been used. (R.J.S.Wiseman)

374 was originally a single deck horse car built by Starbuck in 1877 and given electric equipment in 1906-7 for further service as a works tram, mostly being used as a stores car. Although believed to have been withdrawn in 1951, it was not scrapped until 14 June 1956 in T. W. Ward's yard. Virtually all the trams in stock when the run-down of the system began were scrapped here, except for those few that were preserved (see appendix). (R.J.S.Wiseman)

A total of twelve horse trams were placed on electric trucks, two for further passenger service and the rest as works vehicles, three being ex-company and the others from a batch delivered to the Corporation in 1897 by Milnes. Ex-company car 15 was built by Starbuck in 1874 and converted into the system's sole breakdown car in 1902. In 1946 it was roughly done up to look like a tram of the correct vintage – though it still had its electric truck, motors and controllers – for the Municipal Tramways' Jubilee parade in which it ran as 'horse car 1'. It was then stored at Tinsley before being presented to the Tramway Museum Society (TMS) and is seen here being prepared by society members for shipment to Crich on 21 November 1959. (R.J.S.Wiseman)

The Rotherham tram system was extended to Tinsley, then the municipal boundary with Sheffield, on 21 July 1903. In June 1905 a connection was put in and through services began on 11 September. At the beginning of 1926 ownership of the section between here and Templeborough was transferred to Sheffield, whose 'local' trams worked as far as Vulcan Road, where a siding was opened on 20 September 1927. The scene is very much 'steel city' with major steel mills surrounding the tracks, including Hadfield's East Hecla Works. Many Tinsley cars ran through to here after 11 December 1948. Vulcan Road is empty in this photo, but at shift changes queues would fill the roadside shelters. Today the entire area has been cleared and has become the site of the enormous Meadowhall shopping complex which is emblematic, if anything is, of Sheffield's move from an industrial to a modern retail and commercial centre.

Standard tram 62 is going into Sheffield from Rotherham and is passing the Tinsley branch of the Brightside & Carbrook Co-op which had shops all over the east end of the city as well as a large one on Exchange Street, which after the war moved to Angel Street. Most of this department store was closed in 2008. The west was the preserve of the rival Sheffield & Ecclesall Co-op. The scene is not far away from where Sheffield Road met Bawtry Road, an area now underneath the M1 viaduct. During World War Two headlamps were partially blanked out and fenders painted white and because of invasion fears the name 'Sheffield' was painted over. Loadings were very high during the war and this tram is no exception. A passenger at the time recalled that 'past Attercliffe the road was usually deserted and I became used to the driver's routine of sitting on the stairs eating his sandwiches whilst the tram trundled along by itself'! (W. J. Haynes)

Just a year to go for the Corporation tramways and the crew are taking a break at Vulcan Road. Unless the driver has already changed ends the seat backs will all have to swung before leaving again, a tramcar ritual which always delighted child passengers, especially those who had persuaded their mothers to go for the ride to the terminus and back. This is the lower deck of Standard 210 and shows how comfortable these trams were. Many towns and cities never progressed beyond wooden seating. The conductor is checking his waybill whilst the driver relaxes prior to the long trip back across town to Millhouses. Between the wars, a driver could earn a merit badge plus two shillings extra pay after seven years' safe driving, but he lost it after any accident.

Ticketing throughout the life of the tramway was based on stage fares. The normal thin card tickets dispensed from a rack were used at first and later were replaced by machines using 'Ultimate' pre-printed tickets on paper rolls. Both types of ticket were distinguished by colour and denomination.

By 1934 Rotherham had closed all its internal tram routes and was mostly using trolleybuses. Sheffield refused to allow them in the city so Rotherham Council decided to retain trams on this line only, but bought the new single-ended ones deliberately to resemble trolleybuses. In 1935 Rotherham laid a reversing triangle at the limit of their tracks at Templeborough to accommodate short-workings within the town boundary. The cars did have a back-up controller to assist manoeuvring here, as number 4 is doing. The tram shows signs of wear after heavy wartime use. It seems that the bad blood between the two transport departments wasn't

confined to management. One Sheffield crew taking a break at Tinsley once noticed the preceding car was on fire. The driver put down his can of tea, peered through the window and said, 'Oh, it's only a Rotherham tank – let it burn!'

Between Vulcan Road and Templeborough was a bridge over the railway and canal and in 1948 an aborted pre-war reconstruction scheme was resumed and as a result the through service was suspended on 11 December that year. Supertram now runs underneath the same bridge. Within a few months it was decided not to reopen this section and therefore not to resume the inter-town service as had been originally intended. On 13 November 1949 Rotherham closed its remaining section, partly because of the run-down condition of its cars. This is a pre-war view of a Sheffield tram on the Rotherham terminal circuit in Effingham Street. Trolleybus wiring has been installed so the photo must date from the mid-1930s. 346 had been delivered by Brush as an open-balcony car and then it was fully enclosed after the First World War. The number was later taken by another tram.

The other main tramway branch to the heartland of the heavy steel industry was the Brightside line, opened with horse traction as far as the Wellington Inn on 26 May 1875. It was extended to Brightside Bridge about 1885 where this photograph was almost certainly taken. The building in the background is the Bridge Inn and the few trams were kept in a yard beside it. There was never a stable, though, and the horses must have been walked across to Tinsley. This picture was taken after the Corporation takeover in 1896. The company title has been pasted over and the staff are wearing their new uniforms. (picturesheffield.com)

This crossover just past the junction with Upwell Street was not with a tram line at all but over an industrial railway within the English Steel Corporation plant, used for transferring forgings between one section of the factory and another. Even today this still happens occasionally although road vehicles are now used. On one occasion the works loco ran into a passing tram. This entire 'canyon' of buildings, most of which still stands, belonged to the plant and much still does. The elegant car is probably an Alvis. 512 had a fairly short life, being put into service on 9 December 1950 and scrapped just under a decade later on 27 September 1960, despite every effort having been made to sell these modern cars. (R.J.S.Wiseman)

Brightside must be one of the most misnamed places ever! Most of these factory buildings have gone, those on the left being replaced by modern office suites, but Forgemasters, the successors to English Steel, still use the furthest shed on the right. The 2007 floods brought down part of the retaining wall and damage to the plant as a whole was estimated at £15 million. It was the worst flooding in Sheffield since 1864. The Brightside route replaced a horse service on 26 November 1900 but the old depot at the terminus – no more than a flimsily roofed pub yard anyway – was not reused. The electric trams were withdrawn on 6 December 1958. This picture and the one above were taken during a tramway tour on 15 September 1957. As the tram network shrank enthusiasts took frequent opportunity to hire one or more trams to ride over the remainder of the system. Most of them were organised either by the Light Railway Transport League (LRTL, now Light Rail Transit Association) or latterly by the TMS. (R.J.S.Wiseman)

There are very few photographs of the Petre Street route which had opened on 24 September 1903 and was the first to close, on 19 April 1925. The terminus was at Canada Street. The closely packed terraces are typical of working class housing in northern industrial cities. Bernard Geeson's grocers and off-licence at number 241 retails Stones Ales. William Stones' Cannon brewery was at that time in Sheffield, on Rutland Road, but it closed in 1998. (picturesheffield.com)

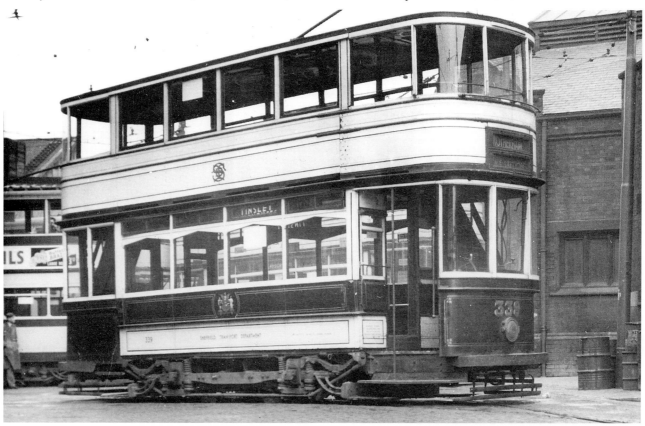

339, though disused, must have lingered at the back of Tinsley Depot where it is pictured on the day it was finally scrapped, 8 February 1957. The Tudor Arch windows on the lower deck were typical of early trams on many systems. The cars were usually known locally as "Prestons". (R.J.S.Wiseman)

The third tram in this High Street line-up is going to Sheffield Lane Top and both the rear ones are from the rocker panel class. The inward curving panels, intended to clear the wheels of horse drawn wagons, were already an archaic feature. Their major disadvantage was that they restricted the width of the saloon and thus the space available for seating.

The Petre Street route ran up from the Wicker along Spital Hill, the name being a reference to the medieval isolation hospital established here well outside the then town limits. This section was shared by the tram line to Pitsmoor, the fourth electric route to open on 27 September 1899, and then extended in stages as far out as Sheffield Lane Top. The gradients meant that services were worked by single deck trams for some years. The ruined church in the background was a Methodist chapel severely damaged in the war and never repaired. It stood on the corner of Burngreave Road and Christ Church Road but Christ Church, rather confusingly, was the Anglican place of worship and was (and still is) at the other end of the street. Roberts car 525 is on the way back towards the city centre and then to Meadowhead; this had been the basic cross-town route worked to and from Sheffield Lane Top since the route was extended to these two outer termini in 1928 and 1934 respectively. (R.J.S.Wiseman)

The 1899 line finished in Pitsmoor. It was extended ten years later further out to Firth Park via Fir Vale. The eventual terminus of the route, Sheffield Lane Top, lay straight ahead up Barnsley Road but lines were never laid along there. St. Cuthbert's Church is on the right here and hidden by the trees on the left is the entrance to the Fir Vale Infirmary (later Northern General Hospital), formerly a workhouse. (R.J.S.Wiseman)

Firth Park takes its name from the open space at its centre. It was designed and laid out in 1874 and then donated to the city in the following year by Mark Firth, a local steel magnate, after which the Prince of Wales (later Edward VII) performed the official opening ceremony. In the early 1950s it was a very well kept public amenity as this view of Standard 229 shows and in recent years a lot of effort has been put into restoring this and many more of Sheffield's fine open spaces. The tram service from Meadowhead via Barnsley Road to Firth Park and Sheffield Lane Top finished on April 3 1960 and was the penultimate closure. The Corporation, incidentally, used the term 'standard' for its trams rather liberally, but 'Standard' in this book refers only to those built in 1928-36, class 10 in the Appendix.

From August 25 1909 the Firth Park terminus was at Bellhouse Road, just in the background of this view. In 1923 a very short extension was constructed to West Quadrant, where the Roberts car is about to reverse in July 1957, this manoeuvre presumably being the reason for the hold up. 513 will return to Woodseats and then via the fine circular line constructed in 1926-27 along Abbey Lane. Various destination screens were used for this particular working. What is displayed here is 'Woodseats and Abbey Lane'. Cars in this direction on the circular route eventually ended up at Tinsley from where they would return to Firth Park. So, unlike Prince of Wales Road, the Abbey Lane service was not a circular one at all, but a wide U-shaped run. (R.J.S.Wiseman)

The third to last extension of the original tramway system was when the Firth Park line reached Sheffield Lane Top on 18 November 1934. This took the trams via Stubbin Lane and back on to Barnsley Road which they already followed through Pitsmoor. This simple view is more emphatically in the past than many others in this book, mainly because of the utter absence of motor traffic. This isn't a busy road even now but it would be next to impossible to find it without cars either passing or parked. In the early 1950s rising costs led to a search for a more economical colour scheme and twenty three trams were repainted in either two-tone or overall green, Standard 221 being one of the latter. Sheffielders made no secret of their disapproval and the cars all reverted to light blue and cream. To balance the books, in 1952 the department reintroduced external advertising for the first time since 1916. (R.J.S.Wiseman)

A local photographer from Firth Park recorded the scene with Standard 189 on the reversing stub at Sheffield Lane Top. Scarcely anything has changed since. The half-timbered Pheasant Hotel is quite a landmark. An oddity, noticeable in later photographs too, is that the tram poles are clearly designed to carry street lights but don't. Instead the old gas lamps, converted with an electric bulb, are all there is. This was quite a busy terminal as three tram routes ran here, the one already described, another via Attercliffe and a part-day service via Savile Street.

Both the other routes back to the city turned off just before reaching Fir Vale and 161 is shown in-bound on the first section along Page Hall Road in 1957. The ramp in the background is Rushby Street and beside it is Owler Lane. A little further down this road joins Upwell Street and in the early 1900s trams from each direction used to turn back here outside the Reform Chapel, which was erected in 1887. Curiously, whilst dogs (even guide dogs) were never permitted on trams or on city bus routes, they were allowed on buses working beyond the boundary. (R.J.S.Wiseman)

From Page Hall Road the tracks ran across to Brightside and the whole was usually referred to as the Upwell Street line. It appears to have opened in two stages on the 9 and 18 August 1902 but the early history of the services using the diversion is not entirely clear. However, single deck trams had to be used owing to restricted clearances under the Upwell Street railway bridge. When work eventually started to lower the roadway, it took nearly two years until through running was resumed on 23 April 1922. This picture is probably of a trial run involving short top cover cars 66 (ER&TC Co.) and 256 (newly built by SCT in 1905). They fitted! The much lowered roadway caused trouble when it flooded. Vera Percy, a passenger during the last war, remembered having to get out and walk through in the blackout to catch another tram on the other side.

After joining the Brightside line at Hawke Street all cars turned towards the city along Brightside Lane. Then the Attercliffe ones turned left along Newhall Road, provided with tram tracks just two days after Christmas Day 1901. 265 is crossing the River Don bridge along here on its way out to Lane Top in May 1957 about five months before this service ceased on 26 October. None of the tracks were abandoned at that stage, though, with the exception of the city terminus at Exchange Street. Two sets of different but interrelated economic changes meant that the industrial premises on the right were empty at the time of writing and the pub across the road was derelict and awaiting demolition. Hammonds Ales were a popular West Riding tipple in the 1950s and 1960s, brewed first at Bradford and then also at Huddersfield and Tadcaster. (R.J.S.Wiseman)

The part-day service continued straight down Savile Street East to the city centre. This bridge crosses Brightside Lane not far below Newhall Road. The very distinctive structure with heavy steel girders supporting the main span still carries the railway tracks towards Doncaster, Barnsley and Leeds. 194 is outward bound to Sheffield Lane Top a couple of years before this route was withdrawn on 28 February 1959. (R.J.S.Wiseman's coll.)

By 1987 the idea of reintroducing trams to the city was beginning to be taken quite seriously. Various studies had been carried out and a bill was placed before Parliament in 1985. In 1987 a public exhibition was held on the Sheffield (Anglican) Cathedral forecourt as a means of gauging public opinion. As part of this the TMS lent their horse car 15 which was displayed under an awning almost where the Supertram stop would eventually go. Just visible at the far end of the paved area is a mock-up of what a modern light rail vehicle might look like; not many Sheffielders knew.

From 10 to 18 December 1990 there was a second exhibition on the Cathedral forecourt which this time included a full-scale mock-up of one section of a Supertram car. Siemens-Düwag built it at a cost of £200,000 and it was unveiled on the 11th by Roger Freeman MP, a Minister in the Transport Department. An important part of the exercise was to receive feedback on the different kinds of seat upholstery provided. The promoters are said to have been taken aback by the fact that the public voted for the most comfortable version! However, it was duly installed and has stood the test of time well partly because, of course, Supertrams have – except for the early days – had conductors.

The real thing! Supertram was extended to the Cathedral stop on 18 February 1995. When the lines were being laid here quantities of human remains were rediscovered, possibly those of paupers buried outside the churchyard proper. When the street was widened in 1890 they had been left undisturbed. The trouble was, the Supertram foundations were deeper than for the former tramways. Screens were erected and the remains taken away for reburial at Abbey Lane Cemetery, at some considerable cost. The overhead standards here are painted in black with gilt lining instead of the more normal blue and grey. Car 114 in the latest (2006) livery is just leaving the Cathedral stop on the route to Middlewood.

The Lloyds-TSB branch on the left occupies the Pawson & Brailsford building, constructed in 1884 in a suitably ecclesiastical style for its position next to the (then) parish church. The opposite building line on High Street was not defined until after 1895 when work finally began to enlarge the medieval street plan. The narrow road was the reason why horse trams were never authorised along here and had to operate in two separate sections. 118 is coming off the most used crossover on the system. It has come in from Herdings Park and is on the part-day service which continues to Meadowhall. These workings run as yellow cars though tram crews often forget to change the display from purple. The horse tramway company had painted its cars in a different colour for each route to aid recognition by the illiterate. It is not clear if Supertram management considers that still to be necessary in Sheffield! But the two successive operators have consistently used a colour identification scheme as opposed to route numbers.

This 1937 postcard view is taken looking down High Street towards Fitzalan Square. The policeman on point duty is controlling the junction between High Street and Angel Street, which had double tram tracks down to West Bar. The buildings on the far side of the street were demolished many years ago to make way for the Arundel Gate dual carriageway, largely the haunt of endless streams of buses today. The outbound line here occupies almost exactly the same space as today's inbound Supertram track. Car 367 was the second to go into service of four experimental trams, 366-369, built by the undertaking between 1918 and 1921, the precursors of the rocker panel class. Series production was left in the hands of outside builders.

The junction with Angel Street was remodelled to form the Castle Square Supertram stop. 103 is seen here pausing at the stop in February 2007 on an evening run to Halfway. Historically Castle Square is incorrect as it was always Market Place; there is even a surviving street plate on one of the buildings in the background to prove it. The medieval castle was actually off Haymarket on the site of the Castle Market. After the war this traffic junction became a roundabout at a cost of £4m and included the usual 1960s underpasses, christened by locals 'The Hole in the Road'. The lighted 'lantern' visible on the top of the building in the extreme background marks out the Telegraph Building, often seen when looking down Fargate. The car is in the 'old' Stagecoach livery applied to the trams from 1998 onwards and phased out from 2006 onwards.

Supertram was opened in stages, as most tramways had been. Test runs were followed by timetabled ghost running in January 1994, then the initial Meadowhall – Fitzalan Square / Ponds Forge segment opened on 21 March. Car 04 is pictured leaving on one of the early morning trips that day. The 'up' line remained fenced off as it was not yet available for use, so cars had to run in 'wrong line' from Park Square and then reverse. By this time temporary screens had been provided for the cars but route indication was confined to boards carried in the drivers' cabs. This was not dissimilar to how the Corporation trams had started in 1899! Some interesting differences from older photographs of this area are the modern Barclays Bank building on the corner of Fitzalan Square and the post-war C&A shop in the background. In the former case the rather handsome domed building was demolished around 1969/70, in the latter the Luftwaffe did the job without reference to the owners.

Later in the day crowds board car 13, anxious to sample the city's latest amenity and almost overwhelming the staff and ticket machines in the process. Many of those visible here were probably recalling the former cream and blue Corporation trams and maybe reflecting how they, the citizens, had so bitterly opposed the bus replacement policy. Initial maps and plans had shown this stop as Commercial Street (where it is placed), but by the time of opening it had become Fitzalan Square/Ponds Forge instead.

This picture of Supertram, about to cross the bowstring girder bridge onto Park Square, was taken on 31 December 1993 whilst trams were still running on test. The former gas company office on Commercial Street is visible on the left of car 1002 (as it was temporarily numbered in Düsseldorf to suit their radio control system) and Ponds Forge international swimming pool, built for the World Student Games, on the right. The hillside was totally transformed in 1957-61 by the construction of the Park Hill Flats complex, described at the time as 'streets in the sky' with decks wide enough for milk floats to deliver to each door. Roy Hattersley was Chair of Housing at the time. The buildings are Grade II listed and are currently being upgraded and restored.

The core of the Supertram system is the Park Square delta junction placed on the enormous roundabout at the point where the Sheffield Parkway funnels traffic on to the inner ring road. Commercial Street, where the tracks ended at this stage, is top left. The incomplete branch at bottom left will go to Halfway / Herdings Park and the Meadowhall line is the one on the right. Look at the gasometers in the background; they are in Neepsend and we shall see them again in connection with the Wadsley Bridge line. In the middle distance is a large market which must have been demolished not long after this picture was taken in December 1993 as a new hotel and offices now occupy the site. Another hotel has replaced the dark block behind the bridge. The tram is just crossing this impressive bridge from Commercial Street on test.

The line between Fitzalan Square and Meadowhall carried its first passenger in March 1994 but the formal opening by HRH The Princess Anne took place on May 25. She unveiled this plaque on Park Square having travelled in on car 12, which did duty as a royal tram that day. Here she is chatting to some of the assembled dignitaries before re-boarding the tram which will take her to the Cathedral stop and the Cutlers' Hall. The Cutlers' Company has been the trade association for the city's industry since 1624. Supertram arrived during a period of immense change. Plant closures and automation had reduced the number of steelworkers in Sheffield and Rotherham from 60,000 to 16,000 over twenty years, even though the area was producing as much steel as it had during the last war. On the other hand the Meadowhall Shopping Centre was expected to have 10,000 employees.

One of the most dramatic structures is the viaduct that carries the trams up the steep hill from Park Square to Cricket Inn Road. Known technically as a balanced cantilever bridge it consists of six spans made from 115 pre-cast units glued together and then stressed by cables running through them in ducts. Most of the surface is paved in case of emergency. The trams have four motors and were specially designed to have all axles motored to cope with Sheffield's hills and they can certainly move on these gradients. This is once again a test run, this time in early 1994. The viaduct here runs alongside the Parkway which is just visible underneath.

The first stop after Park Square – where there isn't one – is Hyde Park and after that it is Cricket Inn Road. There was a temporary Park & Ride site near here between 1994 and 1997 until it was superseded by Nunnery Square. Car 01 – at that time numbered 1001 – is on test there before passenger services began. In the background the cliff face of the Hyde Park Flats dominates the low rise commercial units along the roadside. It is all quite a contrast to the old public house on the left. The tram is outward bound. Traffic on this route received a marked boost because of the legalisation of Sunday trading in the year the line opened.

The depot is at Nunnery Square, originally only a crew halt but upgraded from 12 May 1997 to a passenger stop. Unlike the old style tram depots, where all cars were stored under cover, the Supertrams are stabled outside, with maintenance and repairs carried out inside the shed. The first technicians received about three months training in Düsseldorf. Two trams, as yet unnumbered, stand here on the occasion of a visit by members of the LRTA on 20 November 1993, before the opening. The two-tone grey livery with blue skirt was later completed by small leaf logos on the ends. In 1997 these rather pointless decals were replaced by a bold 'Supertram' logo on the ends and sides together with an exhortation to 'Sit back and relax' and the grey style was finally abandoned in January 1999. The gantry on the right is part of a travelling crane. The building also houses the control centre.

1002 was the first car to be delivered on 26 August 1993. The third – actually number 4 – was delivered to Nunnery Depot on September 23. Like all the others it came by road and sea from the Siemens-Düwag factory in Düsseldorf using a specially built low-loader. Before this some of the trams had been run on test on the light rail system there. The locals christened them 'the whispering trams' and, excellent as most of their own cars are, are said to have demanded to know why they couldn't have similar ones. The 'long' numbers were allotted there and were not intended for continued use in South Yorkshire.

This is the main control panel in the driver's cab. The first four drivers were trained on the modern light rail system in Hong Kong. Drivers' seats had been introduced on the Corporation trams as far back as 1938 but they were little more than stools. Long handles do not have to be twirled today, of course, instead foot pedals cope with many of the jobs, just as they do in a private car. Supertrams are double ended so there is a cab at each end. It was always motormen on the Corporation cars, but one of the earliest Supertram drivers was Julie Crooks who said at the time that she enjoyed 'the job very much and would recommend it to any girl'. Quite a few took up her recommendation.

The saloons have been remodelled since this picture was taken in 1993, principally to improve the facilities for disabled passengers, but the basic layout is still the same. Many trams today are 100% low floor with both level access and a flat floor throughout inside. Because of the need to have all axles motored in Sheffield it was decided to use traditional motorised bogies throughout, two in the centre and one at each end. Each of these is a high floor area therefore. However, both doors at each end lead into a low floor area with ample space for buggies and wheelchairs, plus some seats. There were 88 seats with the original layout, a couple less following the 2006 refurbishment programme. This photo is taken looking from the low floor section to the centre of the car. Longer distance passengers can climb the steps to find ample seating there.

The main function of this line is to serve important non-residential traffic objectives. This would have been less easy, incidentally, had either of the street-based alternatives along Brightside Lane or Attercliffe Road been adopted, as suggested at the start of the design process. Instead part of the trackbed of the freight railway in the foreground, formerly the Great Central line to Rotherham Central, was used from just after Attercliffe to Tinsley. Maximum speed on private right of way is 50 mph (80 kph). This is Arena/Don Valley Stadium which is provided with double length platforms and special access facilities for the two major venues here. Both the stadium (out of sight to the left) and the Hallam FM Arena were built for the 1991 World Student Games. Today they host major sporting events and, in the case of the Arena, also shows. 104 has gone through the 'refresh' process and has the latest blue, orange and red Stagecoach Supertram livery.

The penultimate stop is Tinsley/Meadowhall South. There is pedestrian access to Tinsley and the stop is quite near the original Vulcan Road tram terminus. However most passengers are heading for the shopping centre away on the left. In the background is the famous Tinsley M1 viaduct, a steel structure which was fully refurbished in a two year programme ending in 2007. The line below here was flooded on 25/26 June 2007 and services were curtailed for 24 hours. Behind the viaduct are the Tinsley cooling towers, relics of a long-closed power station, and later something of a symbol for Sheffield. They were not demolished because of fears about the stability of the viaduct. However, in 2008, the current owners, E'on, used more modern methods to bring them down.

And back to the future! 02 stands beside the island platform at Meadowhall on opening day. Normally the yellow route uses this platform face and the purple route the opposite one. All stops have these medium height platforms. As well as a massive shopping centre, Meadowhall is also a transport interchange between tram, bus and rail. It all seems a long time ago as British Rail was still in business and one of their engineers' trains trundles through the station in the Sheffield direction. The tram track between here and Meadowhall South is single, controlled by automatic signals, because the shopping centre would only allocate a narrow strip of land. The oddity that the tram is facing away from the city is accounted for by the fact that the line describes a wide arc immediately after leaving and, once past the viaduct, is safely going the right way.

In 1913, when this view of Fitzalan Square was taken, this track was still only a terminus. It was linked as part of a through route in 1925.. The queuing passengers were kept in order by these metal 'cattle pens'. The most interesting building is the Electra Palace, Sheffield's second purpose-built cinema, which replaced Wonderland. It was constructed in 1911 with a glazed terracotta façade in Fifteenth Century Moorish style. 13 was one of the very first electric trams delivered by Milnes and in all one hundred and twenty-six of the 1899 type had received top covers of this design by 1910; this particular car was scrapped in 1929 without further change. 192, the final single decker built by Milnes, was rebuilt towards the end of World War One as an open-balcony double decker and withdrawn in 1934. The double decker is going to Handsworth.

The first major air raid by the Luftwaffe on 12 December 1940 resulted in severe damage to the city centre, However, it was a Thursday evening, the only time in the week when all the major steel works were shut for maintenance, so casualties were remarkably low, especially as the second big raid followed on the Sunday. On the first occasion fallen power lines left many trams marooned in High Street where flames from the King's Head Hotel set some alight. Only two domed-roof cars were completely written off; this one looks as though it would have been rescued later. Connie Taylor later recalled her experience as a conductress when 'the power went down and we were all shut in the tram for nine hours' and then, she said, they got back to find the depot badly damaged. The man walking past in coat and hat looks completely nonchalant – a perfect example of the legendary British stiff upper lip! The building on the corner of Fitzalan Square in the upper picture opposite is the Marples Hotel. During the raid people took refuge its cellars, but when the building caught fire it collapsed, making escape impossible. Another conductress was encouraged by her driver to take shelter there, but was lucky enough instead to be given a lift to Tinsley in a newspaper van. Over seventy people were killed, the greatest single loss of life in any raid on Sheffield.

Twenty one single deckers, numbers 48,124,127, 156-65, 189-192, 200, 201, 205 and 208 were rebuilt in two batches in this style, in 1906-07 and 1915-18. The first batch had Brush Conaty radial trucks designed to allow the car wheels to pivot in relation to the truck so as to permit longer bodies. None of the competing radial designs were effective in practice as there was excessive wear, so all cars all this class were (re-)equipped from 1915 with Peckham Pendulum P22s (8'6" or 2591 mm) which freed the axles to move laterally independently of the truck frames. Motors and controllers remained unchanged. The second group were vestibuled (i.e. given a windscreen) from the start and the others followed in 1914-16. All were withdrawn in 1933-35. (M.J.O'Connor/NTM)

The Handsworth line turned in the city centre again after 1936, using Leopold Street. This tram, on another service, is passing the Sheffield Assay Office, established in 1773 in order to guarantee the quality of locally made metalware, principally silver. The premises were first on Norfolk Street, then Fargate and moved to this long narrow site between Leopold Street and Orchard Lane in 1881. This was not entirely satisfactorily to the assay master, who lived over the shop, and complained bitterly about the water closets which caused 'a great smell'. There has been at least one move since, to Portobello Street behind West Street, and the building here was demolished. If motor cars were hallmarked, then there should have been no question about the Morris Minor parked opposite, very much a classic model. The tram line along here had been opened at the end of August 1908 with permission at the time restricted to using it as a siding.

Handsworth trams left the town centre via Commercial Street. The smoky Park district, much of it cluttered with old slum properties, was soon to be drastically remodelled by the Hyde Park and Park Hill Flats. The later Standard trams were preceded by a single experimental car, appropriately numbered 1. It was constructed by Cravens in 1927, but the Corporation disputed the cost, so the company received no further orders. Externally the big changes were having straight sides and modifying the control handles to allow the 'banjo' glasses – an extended glass panel – to be dispensed with, giving the car a much more modern appearance. A broad cream band was added below the windows. Inside there were sixty-one upholstered seats throughout, mostly reversible but with some longitudinal benches on each deck, white painted ceilings and better lighting. The car is pictured on 29 April 1956, about a year and a half before it was scrapped. Incidentally, it was the second number 1, as the numbers of scrapped cars were usually re-used; some older cars were also renumbered whilst still in use. (R.J.S.Wiseman)

After briefly touching Sheaf Street Handsworth cars then ran the length of Corn Exchange. At the far end the tracks to the right led to Exchange Street. On the left is Furnival Road (not to be confused with Furnival Street). Corn Exchange, much of which has now disappeared, was named after the building in the background, erected in 1881 by the Duke of Norfolk. Much of it was gutted by a fire in 1947 and the site is now part of the Park Square roundabout. The tram is on the way out to Handsworth via Blonk Street and the Wicker. Oddly enough, these newest trams rarely seemed to look quite as well turned out as the pre-war ones did, it must have been something to do with how rain ran off their streamlined ends. Any tendency to linger and the result was smuts! Just as it was on thousands of washing lines. (R.J.S.Wiseman)

On 12 October 1941 in a final adjustment Handsworth was linked with Crookes. This is the city end of Blonk Street. Osborns was a medium-sized family-controlled steel-making concern and their foundry is in the background just over the Don Bridge. Like Hadfield's and Edgar Allen, one of their products was trackwork. Before new offices were erected here an archaeological dig took place on the site and this revealed the presence of banks of crucible steel furnaces. This process for making high grade steel was invented in the eighteenth century by Benjamin Huntsman of Sheffield, a clockmaker. It was later adapted for large-scale production and the local steelmakers revived it during the last war for armaments manufacture. The crucible process was highly labour intensive so did not survive into the modern era. 202 is running from Handsworth to Crookes on 4 May 1957, the last day of service for this route. At the far end of Blonk Street the building on the left housed Osborns' offices. The view was totally transformed around 2006/7 with new offices and city centre apartments. 18 and 178 were SCT-built Standards, both of which retained a slightly simplified version of the older-style dark blue livery until withdrawal. 18 is going out to Handsworth. (Both R.J.S.Wiseman)

This is the curve from Blonk Street towards Lady's Bridge and, as such, it would not have been used by the Handsworth cars. However, once across the track repairs Standard 156, on the route to Vulcan Road, would have followed the same streets as far as Attercliffe. The cream building in the background is the Lady's Bridge Hotel which was physically attached to the former Exchange Brewery on Bridge Street; maybe there was no need for beer pumps, just a pipe to the vats next door! The brewery was established in 1820 by Tennant Brothers. (R.J.S.Wiseman)

The Handsworth cars passed through Attercliffe where there was a tramway junction with Staniforth Road. In 1957 Attercliffe was a vibrant suburban shopping centre with a large gents' outfitters on the corner here, a Woolworth's and even a department store, John Banner's. Buildings-wise the area has changed very little but a combination of depopulation and competition from supermarkets and Meadowhall has meant that these streets later looked quite run-down in comparison to half a century beforehand. 513 is turning out from Staniforth Road into Attercliffe Road on its way through town to Crookes. It is 3 May and the following day the Handsworth – Crookes route would be closed. (R.J.S.Wiseman)

Not far around this corner were bridges over the canal and a railway. In the latter case it was narrow which meant that, from the inception of the tramway, the tracks had to be interlaced. The canal bridge was raised in 1954 to give greater clearance to barges passing underneath and in 1956 the other bridge was widened. In both cases a temporary single line was laid and at no time was service interrupted and, on completion, double tram track was installed over the railway bridge. Given the fact that all trams were to be withdrawn within a very few years it is remarkable that so much effort was made to achieve this. This is a Roberts car crossing one of the bridges on a journey from the city whilst the work was going on.

At Darnall, Staniforth Road becomes Main Road. Unlike Attercliffe this is still a residential area. After a sharp left turn the track ended here, the branch terminus from 11 April 1901, where 287 is about to reverse. When the tramway was extended beyond here the siding was retained as a short-working point. The picture dates from 19 March 1958 and the route would close less than a month later on 12 April. The streetscape is unchanged and the street paved with the stone setts so typical of northern industrial cities at this period; the odd thing is that these are now the material of choice in the redeveloped areas of the city centre. The Sheffield Tramways Department crest on the top deck sides of the car has been painted out to leave space for advertising. (R.J.S.Wiseman)

Trams reached Handsworth on 29 May 1909 and stopped here at Finchwell Road outside the Norfolk Hotel, still quite recognisable today. However, the street outside the pub was made a dual carriageway many years ago, there is an enormous supermarket across the road and not far to the left of the tram the Sheffield Parkway nowadays carries streams of traffic to and from the M1. 13, an 1899 Milnes tram, would originally have been fitted with a headlamp at the end of its open-top deck. Once these cars were covered and provided with destination blinds it proved to be neater to move the headlamp to the dash. (picturesheffield.com)

The eventual terminus from 7 September 1934 was in Retford Road at Orgreave Lane, a typical area of inter-war semis such as are found on the edges of all towns. This was the main road to Worksop, although road space doesn't seem to be exactly at a premium. A young man is getting himself photographed with the driver. As can be seen, just two trams could be squeezed in to this, the usual layout at a Sheffield terminus. In 1957 William Leigh and his bride took one slot whilst they got married at the nearby St. Mary's Parish Church, after which the nuptial tram took them to the reception in Broomhill; the Suez Crisis meant coach hire was impossible. Handsworth was also the terminus for a large number of workers' specials from Vulcan Road, Brightside and Sheffield Lane Top. All services to Handsworth ended on 4 May 1957.

The Intake route left the city via Broad Street, Commercial Street and Duke Street. 277 is descending the latter about one third of the way down. All the buildings on the right were swept away when the Park Hill Flats were built. The building with the distinctive bay window on the left is Oriel House, premises belonging to C & A Reed, funeral directors, who were established in 1834. The New Inn stands next up on the corner of Bernard Street. The viewpoint from the upper deck of a car going in the opposite direction gives a good idea of how steep the gradient is here. A newspaper columnist in 1960 recalled the pleasure of sitting upstairs at the front 'especially when you were careering down City Road… marvellous'.

This was one of the routes which the Board of Trade, the government regulatory department at the time, decreed had to be worked by single deckers. There is a steady gradient all the way up to Manor Lane, the initial terminus after the line opened on 10 January 1900. The undertaking's first serious accident took place here on 27 March 1902. Single deck car 156 ran out of control from Manor Lane, derailed at the Granville Road junction (ironically, never used) and ended up in the garden of 284 City Road. Despite a full load, fortunately no-one was injured. However, the driver and conductor were found to be negligent and were dismissed.

The top of City Road is often known as Elm Tree. Supertram comes up City Road – behind the photographer – on pretty well the same alignment but turns right not left. The initial plans were to come through the Manor Estate and after that to run for a short distance along Prince of Wales Road as the old trams had done. That might have made more sense from the point of view of passenger traffic, because there would have been a stop at Wulfric Road in the estate. There was a complex junction here with the Prince of Wales Road circular line to the left and it provides an elegant illustration of the skill of the overhead linesmen who would have behind them two or three years at a technical school and an engineering apprenticeship. With trolley-equipped tramways the wire had to be carefully positioned so as to follow the centre-line of the car. With the more modern bow collectors, used in cities such as Leeds and Glasgow, this was less important.

Woodhouse Road was reached on 17 April 1902. Woodhouse, about a mile away down the road to the right, was not within the city boundary at that period and even Intake looks quite rural. 58 was built by the ER&TC Co. who provided a distinctive style of current collector. Most single deckers simply had a very long trolley pole, but this car has a shorter one atop a vertical post. The strong springs to hold the pole down are visible at the top of the post. Open-fronted trams were no joke. Driver William Davis recalled that 'you didn't grow a moustache because it would freeze. You wore Danish clogs if you could afford them and coats

and capes but you still prayed it would not rain'. A driver's daughter remembers her dad coming home with his face bleeding after being cut by hailstones. How pleased he was to get enclosed cars which he called glasshouses or ships. (A.D.Packer's coll.)

The route was extended the short distance to Hollinsend Road on 8 February 1935 and then to Birley Vale on 29 December; this was the final extension of both this route and of the system as a whole. It has always been a somewhat desolate spot. An intensive workmen's service ran every day to and from here and Elm Tree at shift change times, mostly from Brightside or Vulcan Road. The earliest morning car left at 5.00 and the last evening one at 10.08. The all-day service always ran to Walkley. The tramway clock tells us that it is precisely midday. Closure was a two stage affair. On 7 April 1956 the direct service along City Road was withdrawn, but then for a few months until 6 October the normal workers' services to the East End continued and an all-day route from Fitzalan Square via Prince of Wales Road was added. Car 82 was scrapped five months after this last date.

The Prince of Wales Road line opened on 24 February 1928, but this picture was taken on 12 April 1958, the day all services ceased along this fine tramway. It is 11.10 at night. One tram is pictured waiting to leave the terminus at Fitzalan Square for Darnall & Intake (Elm Tree), the other for the Beaumont Road crossover, a regular short-working point about half way up Prince of Wales Road. Both would then have travelled via Attercliffe, as the City Road line had been closed two years earlier leaving the Prince of Wales route as an out-and-back service rather than a full circle. (R.J.S.Wiseman)

Sharply increased traffic in a city so essential for the war effort meant that, even without the air raid losses, more trams were urgently required. New ones were out of the question so sources for second-hand ones were trawled. Between 10 October and 4 November 1941 fourteen surplus Hurst Nelson open-platform Class A cars dating from 1901 arrived from Newcastle-upon-Tyne. During 1941-42 Queens Road fully enclosed them and painted them in pre-1928 style but using the lighter blue. They seated sixty and were renumbered 311-324. These cars were withdrawn over 1948-1952. 313 is shown here in Fitzalan Square, one of two to receive longer 7'0" (2134 mm) trucks. Like all except three of the cars it had no end destination indicators. The preceding car is going to Intake via Darnall and the circular line.

The new line branched off at a junction with the Handsworth route in Darnall. Near the end of a short street section the track was laid through the bridge carrying the former Great Central Railway to Worksop, currently served by Northern Rail trains. The all-day tram service was a complete circle, starting from City and running out via either Darnall or City Road and back by the other route. Many works specials worked along here too. Remarkably the station at Darnall is still open in 2008, though it sees few passengers and no long goods trains pass since the closure of virtually all of South Yorkshire's and North Nottinghamshire's coal mines.(R.J.S.Wiseman)

This shot gives a good impression of the superb reserved track line, which was longer and more important than the Abbey Lane circular. It was built to serve the Manor housing estate, seen here in the background, but also dealt with very intensive workers' services to and from the steelworks. Community amenities were planned in to the development, including schools, churches and, in the left background here, shops. This is Fairleigh near the top of the line and demonstrates the way the track was laid in the median strip of the dual carriageway, anticipating one of the features of modern light rail.

The Halfway line is the longest of the three main Supertram routes This early shot in August 1992 shows the construction of the bridge from the Park Square junction towards the railway station. The Park area rises up the hill behind with the Park Hill Flats on the right and the Hyde Park Flats on the left. Towering above them is the abandoned remnant of a block under demolition. The tall chimney is not some relic of heavy industry but serves a district heating plant.

123 stops on an inward-bound trip at Sheffield Station/Sheffield Hallam University on 4 May 2007. The stop name is a bit optimistic, because although the station is just beyond the wall the university is the jumble of buildings on the hillside, much of it up a steep climb. It has to be admitted that buses serve the campus better. The wavy roof to the right is the new overbridge built as part of the 2006 station revamp. Because of this the former tram stop 100 yards nearer Park Square was replaced by this new one and it does provide good interchange. An electronic departure indicator at the top of each stairway within the station would be an ideal way to advertise the presence of the connecting tram service. Maybe when Supertram gets real time information screens that might be a possibility.

Here is a car on the viaduct taking trams up towards Norfolk Park, just after the stop at Granville Road/Sheffield College. It was necessary to build the viaducts here and up to Hyde Park on the Meadowhall branch to avoid exceeding the maximum gradient the trams were designed to cope with. In this case also it means that the tramway can be squeezed in to a narrow strip above the main railway line to London and then cross Norfolk Park Road on the bridge rather than at grade. Drivers are able to accelerate uphill too without needing to be concerned about other road traffic.

Before trams first ran up here, this Heath Robinson contraption was being used by Balfour Beatty to put the finishing touches to the overhead wiring along Park Grange Road. The trolley is not electrically powered of course, the pantograph is just to check that all the adjustments have been made correctly so that the first passenger-carrying trams will have a trouble free run through. The tower was built to the Supertram gauge so that all clearances with poles could be checked. A problem in this particular area was that, almost as the tramway was opened, the council demolished three tower blocks, the inhabitants of which had been factored in to the traffic forecasts. However, some very nice new houses have been built since. This long route was opened in stages with the first segment being Fitzalan Square to Spring Lane (City Road) on 22 August 1994 with this short section serving new stops at the station, Granville Road, Park Grange and Arbourthorne. This view is looking from the temporary terminus down Park Grange Road. In the next stage trams will continue past the photographer to join City Road which had been used nearly fifty years earlier by trams to Intake. At first Supertram tickets were issued by agencies (more cheaply) or from machines (unfortunately behind the tram here) sited on each platform. Sheffielders confessed themselves bemused by this new idea! It wasn't helped by having to cancel each ticket in a separate machine, also on the platform. On July 17 1997 conductors were introduced on all trams after a period of experimentation. Ticket machines remained in situ for a while and pre-purchased tickets still had to be cancelled before boarding. However the final changeover was not long delayed and this boosted people's confidence in using the system.

This is the scene in July 1993 as the Supertram tracks are being constructed on City Road. The basis is a deep concrete foundation on top of which a metal mat was laid to arrest any stray currents and then finally came a reinforced concrete slab laid with grooves ready for the rails. The slab was produced using a slip-form paver, a machine usually used for roads or airport runways and not normally adapted for producing a grooved form like this. However, it was more than twice as fast as manual methods would have been. The total infrastructure expenditure was £119 million whilst the fleet of twenty five cars cost £42 million. A red Thompson Travel bus on service 294 passes the excavations on the way towards the Interchange.

The way traditional tramways usually dealt with short workings was to have a conveniently placed crossover where trams could reverse. Idsworth Road in Fir Vale was a good example. This was fine when there wasn't much road traffic. Occasionally, however, a siding would be laid off the main road, like at Vulcan Road. Supertram has adopted this method in two places, Malin Bridge and Herdings Park. The latter branch, which was opened on 3 April 1995, leaves the through route at Gleadless. It does have one intermediate stop on it, but it is little more than a glorified siding. The original plan was to make it single track but the Council insisted on double line. This stop is at Leighton Road and the traffic potential is obviously not high.

Supertram leaves the city via Commercial Street, just as the Intake trams did, but after that follows an entirely different route past the station and Park Grange Road before joining City Road about two thirds of the way up it. This final stretch to Elm Tree is the only place where the Halfway line follows the course of the old tramway. However, no stop was provided on City Road on the insistence of the City Council. 111 climbs towards Manor Top (also known as Elm Tree) on 9 May 2007. The Supertrams came from Siemens AG, Germany who had only recently bought out the famous Düsseldorfer Waggonfabrik (always known as Düwag), so the bodies had their maker's plates (though they seem to be disappearing with the recent refit). The electrical gear was from Siemens proper. Düwag had offered a wide variety of models so cars were usually built using a

good deal of hand labour. Incidentally, their factory was used during World War II to make V1 and V2 rockets, just as Sheffield factories were also largely turned over to war production. The next step on 5 December 1994 took trams via Manor Top/Elm Tree and Hollinsend to Gleadless Townend. This is on part of the outer ring road and continues the line of Prince of Wales Road, once also home to a tramway. After this the line turns off the ring road and a gyratory system means there is a short length of what tramway enthusiasts used to call 'Cannon-Hilling' after an area in Birmingham where the lines were laid on parallel streets. 124 is running out of town along Gleadless Road here.

109 stands at the final stop on the Herdings Park branch during the winter of 2007 in a light dusting of snow. The disappearing tower block issue arose here too, but some of the blocks were only emptied in order to refurbish them (this happened on Norfolk Park too). By February 2007 people were back home and more were using the tram.

The land that the Mosborough and Halfway Townships were built on was part of Derbyshire until a boundary change during the last century and the line still passes briefly through that county between the White Lane and Birley Lane stops. Halfway became the final terminus on 27 March 1995. The track here is exactly like so many of the old Corporation tram termini, just a double line ending in a single track reversing stub. That worked in 1900 and it works now. The stop is laid out next to a roundabout in a fairly desolate patch of ground surrounded by roads, housing estates and commercial premises. At least that makes plenty of space for the Park & Ride site on the right of the picture. A major aim and success of the tramway has been the attraction of motorists on to the trams as a means of limiting traffic congestion in the city centre.

FITZALAN SQUARE, SHEFFIELD.   C.533.

This postcard view of Fitzalan Square was probably taken in the 1930s. The redesigned central island had been opened in 1909 by the Lord Mayor, the Earl Fitzwilliam; his family, one of the wealthiest in England, lived at nearby Wentworth Woodhouse and owned considerable property in Sheffield. The statue of Edward VII was erected in 1913 and is the only royal memorial left in the city centre. The postcard was not posted until 1943 after many of the surrounding buildings had been destroyed in air raids. C&A in the left background was a casualty, but was rebuilt fairly quickly in a similar style, albeit without the tower. The taxi rank had replaced the Hansom cab stand and new concrete passenger shelters were erected. Despite the early rejection of the central interchange here the square was always used as a terminus by several services, the last one not being withdrawn until 1959. (G. Smith coll.)

Flat Street, the short road between Fitzalan Square and Pond Street, is a nineteenth century addition to the street plan. For a few years the lines formed a siding used as part of the terminal layout, but on 19 May 1904 they were extended down Pond Street to the Midland Station junctions, although initially the tracks were only used for depot access. 295, built in 1912, is shown entering Flat Street in 1932.
(M.J.O'Connor/NTM)

Pond Street takes its name from medieval ponds on this low-lying site below the castle. From late 1939 a peak period service used the track in one direction and from 12 October 1941 Woodseats and Wadsley Bridge were combined in one route via Pond Street. On a cold day in February 1956 car 77 is on a short-working from Woodseats to Fitzalan Square and a bus is pulling out of the bus station where covered stands were provided for the first time that year. Half a century on, the original proposed scheme for a central terminus was taken up, but for buses rather than trams. However, it has never been very convenient for the city centre. The former jumble of commercial premises has been cleared and in the background one of the new Polytechnic buildings is in the course of construction. Nikolaus Pevsner, the architectural historian, thought these rather utilitarian blocks made successful use of the steep site and they later came to form part of the Hallam University Campus. (R.J.S.Wiseman)

At the far end of Pond Street is Leadmill Road, where this superb night time shot of the permanent way gang relaying the track was taken on 15 March 1955. Unlike some smaller tramways which became totally decrepit before being put out of their misery, Sheffield retained high standards almost until the final closure. The line along here to Queens Road Works was left in until the last, in 1960, but even so the points would have had plenty of wear left in them. Hopefully they were lifted and donated to a museum tramway. At Crich Tramway Museum they only began to run out of salvaged components half a century after the last UK tramway closures. (R.J.S.Wiseman)

Shoreham Street Depot, nearby, was opened in 1911 and closed on 28 February 1959. It later became Leadmill Bus Garage and was retained by Mainline until the mid-1990s. Afterwards the site was cleared and redeveloped but even then this entrance, which has small turrets on either side, was allowed to stand as a reminder of the tramway era. 119 is a wartime replacement for a Standard tram destroyed in the blitz. The conductor is following his car into the shed. Tram crews tended to regard themselves as a bit above bus men. Even in October 1959 when bus crews went on strike it took a day for staff on the two remaining tram routes to come out in sympathy. Towards the end of the 1990s Mainline was sold to First Group, so after Stagecoach took on Supertram these two major transport concerns became competitors within Sheffield, especially after Stagecoach added the Yorkshire Traction bus company to their portfolio.

Five types of works tram were operated during the life of the system, breakdown, salt, stores, snowplough and water cars. A total of sixteen 1899-pattern single and double deck passenger trams were converted to works cars. 361 had been a 1900 Brush single decker; its body was shortened by one bay on conversion. 357 was also by Brush but a double decker built in 1904; its flat roof shows how the upper deck had been sliced off. The cars are having a rare outing into the sun outside Shoreham Street Depot. Most works cars were snowploughs. Only the legendary 1947 winter defeated them when the hard-packed snow meant that the wheels could not make electrical contact with the rail. Supertram has no separate works cars, but when it snows trams run 24 hours to keep the tracks clear and one or two can be fitted with small snowploughs as well. (R.J.S.Wiseman)

The petrol station and garage in the background was owned by Kenning, a well-known motor chain at the time; this building was later converted into an arts centre which includes the Showroom Cinema. The overhead line crew were soon to be out of a job, but on 27 March 1960 they were still available to fix a defective trolley head on Roberts car 518 just outside the former depot. By and large overhead line work was not something that a works tram was suitable for, because the likelihood was either that the power was off or that there was a blockage on the line. The only case when railed equipment was usually necessary was where there was a lot of reserved track, and this was not the case in Sheffield. One of these motor tower wagons is preserved at Crich. (R.J.S.Wiseman)

The Woodseats route was unique for Sheffield in that alternate trams left the city via different lines in Shoreham Street and Queens Road, though the earliest this can have applied was 1904. Next to Queens Road some temporary wooden sheds were built in 1900-1901 as a running depot with the permanent buildings completed in 1905. In the photograph, 112, a Brush 1899-pattern car, is still in largely original condition with open-top and roof-mounted headlamp. The only change has been the substitution of a route blind for the route letter box carried until about 1905. The fairly spartan seating consisted of longitudinal benches in the saloon and reversible 'garden seats' upstairs, all of course made of wood.

1913

Above: Once Shoreham Street Depot opened it was possible to close the running shed at Queens Road and to transfer the works there from Nether Edge, which was then closed. Sixty new balcony roof trams with enclosed platforms were built in 1913-15 by Brush (296-345) and SCT (346-355), the latter in the new Queens Road Works. There were fifty-eight seats. Sixteen 1899-pattern cars were rebuilt like this in 1913-19, all except three having already received short canopy top covers. 179, which had been fully enclosed in 1919, appeared with open-balconies in 1928 but 296-349, 351. 354 and 355 were fully enclosed in 1919-22. The remaining eighteen open-balcony trams were withdrawn in 1929-1935. This is an official photograph illustrating the contrast between the old and the new designs. Car 6, which was later altered again with an open platform, was the car chosen.

Above left: A large series of class B single truck cars were built for the London County Council Tramways in 1903, but by World War One all were standing out of use due to staff shortages. Sheffield bought twenty in 1917-18 and numbered them 356-65, 56 (128 in 1924), 94 (90 in 1925), 125, 129, 187, 188, 203, 207, 209 and 210. The cars entered service in the LCC livery. Rotherham Corporation also purchased some at the same time and converted theirs to open-balcony cars in 1922, six of these being transferred to Sheffield in 1926 (numbered 91-6). All the class had been withdrawn by 1931. Pictures of the cars in service are rare and 188 is seen outside Queens Road. (R.J.S.Wiseman's coll.)

Queens Road joins Shoreham Street just before the junction with London Road which is in the background here. The rank of shops to the rear has hardly changed, but on the right one can now look across and see the impressive minaret of a newly-built green-domed mosque, also visible from trains as they approach Sheffield Station. The gents' convenience on the corner is now boarded up; modern man and woman must be gifted with a self-control denied to the wartime generation. 289 is about to join London Road on its journey to Woodseats Terminus.

It seems highly likely that the second of these two photographs was taken as a 'then and now' contrast with the first. Both the Heeley and Nether Edge horse tram routes opened in 1877, respectively on 29 October and 24 December, thus completing the company system. The first picture shows car 33, bought that year, at the Albert Road terminus in Heeley. It appears in its newly-applied livery and lettered for the places served, as was usually the case for horse trams. The window sticker for Lewis's gas mantles, repeated on the hoarding, is perfectly in period. Burnetts coal could be had from Park Street Station, which was a city centre goods terminal on a spur from the former Great Central line just beyond Victoria. The company evidently brought their new car out from the nearby depot for this posed shot. The Corporation did likewise after their takeover in 1896 and used the same tram. The Company title was painted or pasted over. Private concerns rarely wasted money on uniforms, but councils thought them a matter of municipal pride. The advertisement panels on the upper deck panels this time include Zebra, a black leading for the iron firegrates found universally in both working class and middle class homes, and Reckitt's Blue, a wash whitener particularly necessary in a smoky industrial city. Reckitt and Nestles are both still in business today. (2nd pic. M.Jones coll.)

The Heeley horse tram depot was not converted for electric cars in 1901 and rather miraculously survived intact. It is just possible to see from this view that there were three stable blocks compared to one small two-road car shed (out of sight). In effect, the stables were the power station and many more horses were needed than trams. The latter could run all day, but the horses could manage only a few hours at a time. The men too had to work a great deal longer than their equine charges. At the Corporation takeover in 1896 the average working week for platform staff was a staggering 102 hours. Eventually the depot complex was Grade II listed and recent redevelopment into flats has preserved the depot arch and two of the stable blocks, whilst the third has been opened out to form a paved garden area.

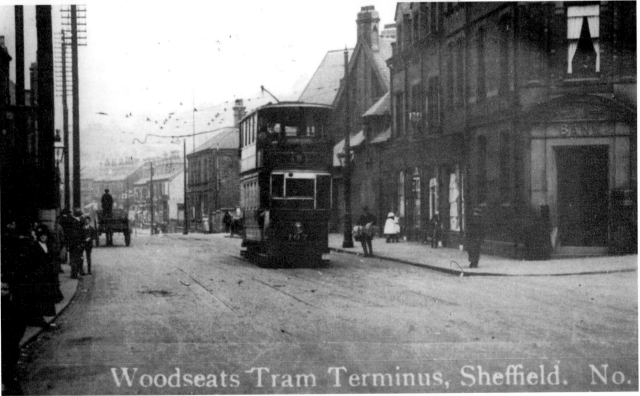

Woodseats Tram Terminus, Sheffield. No.

Electric trams reached Lowfields on 1 August 1900, Albert Road (the horse terminus) on 1 November 1900, and Woodbank Crescent exactly two years later. By 6 April 1903 the lines extended to Chantrey Road. This side street is named after Sir Francis Chantrey (1782-1841). the most famous artist to have come from the area. Although he did paint he was most renowned as a sculptor. 107 was an original Brush tram, first given one of the Sheffield-style short top covers and then appearing as an open-balcony car around World War I. This interesting picture must have been taken around that time, as the route was extended again in 1923. However, this interim terminus was in use for twenty years and the scene is not that different today. (R.J.S.Wiseman's coll.)

The trams were extended to a stub terminal in Abbey Lane from 22 January 1923. This particular crossover was probably added as part of the 1927 circular line. After that closed in February 1959 the track was left at Woodseats for a further seven months for the remaining cars running to or from Wadsley Bridge. This photograph was taken a couple of months before that service ended on 3 October. The crossover was outside the Abbey Lane School which dated from 1928 at a time when Sheffield was expanding in this direction. Bus 471 is picking up passengers

on route 63 which had replaced the Abbey Lane circular tram route in the clockwise direction. Buses running out via Millhouses and Beauchief used the number 61. 'It was', the Chairman of the Transport Committee said, 'imperative that we should move with the times by substituting buses for trams'.

On 12 July 1928 a further length of track was opened from Woodseats out to Meadowhead. The Sheffield Lane Top service was extended here, though some cars from Meadowhead terminated at Sheaf Street. In the background is the Midland Station which has for many years been the only main line station in Sheffield, except that more recently one or two London trains have started calling at Meadowhall on their way to and from Barnsley. Judging by the rather splendid array of motor cars parked across the street this is a pre-1939 view, especially as the jumble of industrial buildings behind the tram are still standing. 449, a Brush-built rocker panel car, part of a series delivered in the period 1919-1922, must have just reversed on the crossover here. The destination screen for Meadowhead was sometimes written in this distinctive style with a large size 'O'.

Just above the railway station was a complex tramway junction from which began a single and loop line along Paternoster Row and Furnival Street through to The Moor. It had been opened on 25 January 1904 to provide a route by which works specials could avoid the congested city centre streets and, for a very short time, a city circular service. Meadowhead cars did not normally use it, but they did reach either end. The original layout was never altered so enthusiasts' tours rarely missed the chance to run along it. One was arranged on 28 April 1957 to say farewell to the last survivors of the rocker panel class, 42, 52 and 497, all visible in this shot at Eyre Street. Both street names, and Norfolk Street nearby, recall the period when Sheffield was a seigneurial borough with certain privileges reserved to its lords, from the 13th century the de Furnivals, followed by the Earls of Shrewsbury and finally the Dukes of Norfolk. Vincent Eyre was an agent to the Duke. When regular services ceased on 4 January 1958 most of the rail was lifted but the double track and junction into The Moor at the top was left in place. It was used for the final time on 17 May 1958 when the Queen Mother visited the city. It was feared that her trademark high heels might catch in the tram tracks and so these were covered over. All the southern routes had to reverse at Moorhead. 247, coincidentally a Meadowhead car, has done so at Union Lane beside the offices and showroom of Newton Chambers & Co. Ltd. of Chapeltown, one of the most interesting Sheffield manufacturers at that time. They had mined their own coal up to Nationalisation and produced everything from massive steel fabrications down to fire grates, including the ironwork for London's Tower Bridge. One of their chemists discovered Izal disinfectant, derived from coal tar, and they also built tanks and Bailey bridges during the war. (Both R.J.S.Wiseman)

This does not have to be a Meadowhead car, but the cross-city service used The Moor, as did cars running beyond Woodseats along Abbey Lane. This late-1930s view shows one of the domed- roof cars which were built in 1936-39. This one is almost new with cream roof and Sheffield Transport Department monogram on the top deck side. Much of The Moor was destroyed in the Blitz and afterwards rebuilt in post-war 'concrete box' style. A man born on the street about 1920 recalled how 'at night all the trams [passed] up and down, there wasn't a lot of cars on the road them days... at Christmas it was a gorgeous sight, that Sheffield Moor, beautiful'. Fifteen years later motor traffic was already

becoming quite significant, although you wouldn't see a motorcyclist riding without a helmet today. Nobody would describe the post-war street as anything other than utilitarian. Much of it is currently being redeveloped once more.

The Meadowhead extension began where Woodseats cars turned into Abbey Lane. The curve in the foreground leading to Abbey Lane was used for just one school special a day. The brick-built church top right is Roman Catholic and dedicated to Our Lady of Beauchief and St Thomas (à Becket) of Canterbury, recalling the dedication of the Premonstratensian Abbey founded along Abbey Lane at Beauchief about 1175. The tower of the abbey survives together with a seventeenth century chapel built from some of the remaining stones. The junction was the scene of a collision between a tram and a coal lorry whose brakes had failed. Both careered into a shop front and coal poured through the tram's broken windows. 'I saw two small legs sticking up out of the coal', the driver said, 'and pulled [a] child out dazed and black as the ace of spades.'

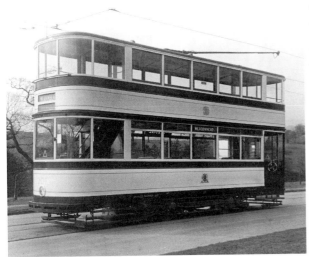

The terminus was a favourite location for official photographs as Graves Park provided a fine backdrop. Standard tram 207 was delivered on 25 February 1935. Just beforehand cars 202 and 203 had appeared in two experimental liveries using a new lighter blue and much more cream; this second version became the norm thereafter. The big changes from the rocker panel class were the elimination of the in-swept panels and modifying the control handles to allow the 'banjo' glasses to be dispensed with, giving the car a much more modern appearance. The Standards had the same equipment as experimental car 1, namely Peckham P22 8'6" (2591 mm) trucks, MV 102DR 50HP motors and BTH B510 controllers. Most cars were built in-house (2-35, 61-130, 156-230 & 243-248) except for 131-155 which were contracted out to Hill's of South Shields. This firm went bankrupt whilst delivery was under way but the receiver ensured that the order was completed. Nine cars were destroyed during the war and the remainder were withdrawn in 1951-60, one or two thus seeing out the system.

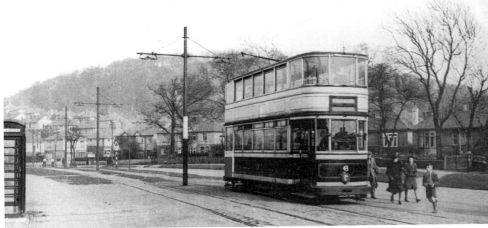

A little more than a year before the Meadowhead extension was opened, on 12 July 1928, Woodseats was linked with Millhouses by a new circular route, mostly along Abbey Lane. Here the reservation was on grassed track between a service road and the main carriageway. Both reserved track routes allowed the use of centre poles for the first time since the Edwardian era. Meadowhead is in the background and car 6 is going to Firth Park via Millhouses and Pitsmoor. The date is probably 1947, a deduction borne out by the styles of the passengers clothes. The rear dash of car has been hastily repainted in a grey undercoat, a sign of the post-war shortages which made it difficult for Queens Road to make up for wartime maintenance arrears. All services along Abbey Lane were withdrawn on February 28 1959.

Beauchief (pronounced 'Beechiff' in Sheffield) is the name the twelfth century monks gave to their new home and it means 'beautiful headland'. It became part of the tram network when the Abbey Lane circular was opened on 14 April 1927. As can be seen here the line to Millhouses was also formed on roadside reservation and this section was retained when the rest of the route was abandoned. When the tramway did become disused in 1960 it was not long before it was added to the road which then became a dual carriageway as a result. The tram is about to turn across and into Abbey Lane. The passenger shelter here was a particularly elegant example. After the last war 191 was one of twenty three Standards virtually taken apart and given new lower saloons resembling those of the more modern domed-roof cars. The Abbeydale Industrial Hamlet, an important early crucible steel works, is a little way down the main road from here.

Millhouses was first served by trams from 17 April 1902, but the route had been extended a short distance from Millhouses Lane to the Wagon & Horses – just across the road on the right – on 31 July 1926 just before it was connected to Abbey Lane. However many cars from Tinsley still reversed, first using a crossover and then later in 1927 the turning loop, over on the left. There were only two European-style turning circles on the system – the other, far less intensively used, was at Rustlings Road near Hunters Bar – and this one provided excellent off-road space for waiting trams. The car is taking the points into the loop which exited on the far side of the waiting room in the background. 32 has just enjoyed a fresh coat of paint because in the early 1950s it was one of those cars experimentally turned out in a short-lived green livery. In 1946 celebrations were held to mark the Golden Jubilee of the Corporation Tramways. Queens Road built a completely new tramcar, and just as the domed-roof cars had epitomised the Thirties, so 501 represented the spirit of the Forties and Fifties with its elegant streamlined body outline, described at the time as 'right up to 1946 motor-coach Standards'. Because of postwar shortages the body used ash rather than teak. The upper deck had no bulkheads or staircase screens, made possible because of the platform doors. Uniquely for the time it had fluorescent lighting and came into service on 12 August 1946. Very few British towns in the post-war period, with the exception of Blackpool, can have had postcard makers anxious to illustrate their trams, but here is the Jubilee car at the turning loop. (2nd pic. G. Smith coll.)

The junction between Abbeydale Road on the right and London Road on the left. The spire belongs to Highfield Trinity Methodist Church not, as might be imagined, an Anglican building; in fact, the nearby St. Barnabas' Church amalgamated with Trinity many years ago. The hotel on the corner site has now closed and been turned into the Royal Apartments. The contemporary Rover parked beside the pole on the right kept up the marque's reputation for style as did the more recent Rover 75, but the latter was probably the last of the line.

The top end of The Moor used to be known as Moorhead, prominently marked by the Crimean Monument, atop which was Queen Victoria at her imperial best. On the left are the premises of T & G Roberts the drapers, built in 1882 and destroyed in 1940; after the war the firm built a new department store further down The Moor, but this closed many years ago. Millhouses trams passed this point and number 196 is on that route, denoted by a letter M at this early period. Car 18 is returning from Heeley on route H; the same letter was also used for Hillsborough. 196 was one of the first six double decker trams constructed by the Corporation itself at Nether Edge Works. Before that two experimental single deck cars had been built, one having been destroyed by fire and the other fairly quickly converted to a works car. (M.Jones coll.)

63

Pinstone Street runs between The Moor and Fargate and was also used by route M. This Edwardian postcard view shows the Town Hall, opened in 1897 by Queen Victoria from her open carriage; she was too old by then to climb the steps to the entrance. In front of it is St. Paul's Church, a fine Baroque style building dating from the early eighteenth century. The dome was added in 1768. It was arguably Sheffield's best single building, but was demolished in the late 1930s to make way for public gardens. These Peace Gardens, as they are known, later became a much appreciated public amenity. Car 75 is going to Millhouses. The fancy scroll work on the overhead poles adds the final touch to this pleasing scene.

In the 1930s the top end of Fargate was known as Town Hall Square. The junction on the left is with Leopold Street. The island with the rock garden on it marks the site of a police kiosk which was manned between 1930 and 1933 to enforce a one way traffic scheme in Pinstone Street, intended for the benefit of the trams. The street then became two way once again. The spire is of St. Marie's RC Church (later Cathedral) on Norfolk Row. The two types of Standard tram are visible here, the rear car being Brush-built 47, which was scrapped in February 1954. (M.Jones coll.)

Part of the 1930 reorganisation involved the relocation of tram stops formerly in Fargate to Pinstone Street. The passenger shelters were built up against the wall of St. Paul's Churchyard, despite the protests of the vicar. Rather illogically, once the third loading track was laid alongside the shelters the one way system was immediately discontinued, meaning that trams stopping here conflicted with other road traffic. The centre track was used for cars that had halted beforehand to overtake those stopping here and though it became redundant after the closure of the Ecclesall to Middlewood route on 27 March 1954 it remained usable right up until the end. The picture was taken in the course of the rocker panel tour already referred to and shows cars 52 and 497. (R.J.S.Wiseman)

The Smith's Crisps van is parked about halfway along Fargate just before a shop belonging to Robert Proctor & Sons. They were drapers, a type of retail outlet that has entirely disappeared to be replaced by the various chain stores. The low-rise buildings to the right have also gone. The tram was originally car 59 in a series of 1899-style cars provided by the Electric Railway & Tramway Carriage Works Co., Preston. It became one of sixteen cars rebuilt with enclosed vestibules and open-balconies in 1913-1919 and was renumbered to 87 in 1924. This class of tram had been withdrawn by 1935. (M.Jones coll.)

The white Telegraph Building shown in this 1930s view was built in 1916 as Kemsley House and named after the paper's publisher. The portico was topped by a figure of Mercury, the messenger of the gods. On the left hand side is Cole Brothers, a local department store and city institution; the location was always known as Cole's Corner. Immediately opposite, the ornate clock marks the end of a narrow side street, Chapel Walk, which leads through to Norfolk Street, though sadly today without the benefit of the clock. 338 and 481 pass on the curve into Fargate from High Street. The former was built by Brush around 1914 as a balcony car and was enclosed after 1919 whilst 481 was a Cravens rocker panel car built towards the end of the production run of this type. (M.Jones coll.)

The axis between the High Street end of Fargate and the bottom of The Moor was used by a large number of tram routes. The Nether Edge line was part of the first electric tram route between there and Tinsley, but in the event the through service lasted just one day, the two terminals later being linked to other destinations. This picture at Cole's Corner was taken on the day of the visit of King Edward VII to Sheffield. Throughout the city centre the buildings were a perfect riot of garlands, bunting and patriotic flags. Number 38 was the final

double decker in the first batch of Milnes cars. After some years running with a top cover it was sold to the Gateshead Tramway Company with seven other cars in 1922, including 74; the lower deck of this one survived and formed the basis for the restoration of a car of this type in the Crich museum workshops.

Horse trams from Nether Edge and Heeley ran only as far in as Moorhead. The street was then known as South Street, Moor, and the photograph was taken in 1887 at the time of Queen Victoria's Golden Jubilee. The large banner was the contribution of John Atkinson, draper, a firm which retained its independence and built a new department store in much the same location on The Moor after the Second World War. This is car 12 built in 1887 by the Ashbury Railway Carriage & Iron Co. and was one of two to have had forward-facing garden seats on the top deck rather than the more usual knifeboard type. A single deck horse car and bus pass in the background. Both the Nether Edge and Heeley routes used The Moor. (picturesheffield.com)

One has to be quite sharp-eyed to spot that this photograph was taken not in the late nineteenth but the mid-twentieth century. This, however, is 1961. After it went to Crich car 15 was fitted with an ex-Glasgow horse car truck. It was then returned to Sheffield where the Corporation restored and repainted the body and the tram was actually horse-hauled along The Moor during the 1961 Christmas season using the electric tram lines near Ellin Street which were still down at the time (according to source this happened for just two hours on Sunday 3rd December). It was, and will almost certainly remain, the last tram along this thoroughfare. although in its first incarnation this tram would not have run along here.

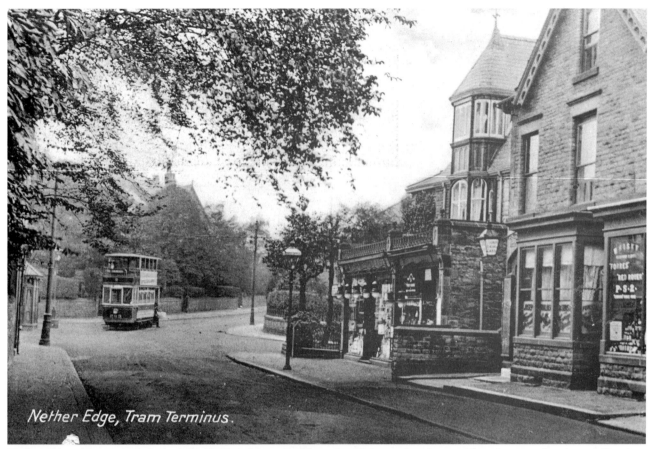

Nether Edge, Tram Terminus.

Nether Edge, like a good deal of Sheffield, is blessed with a plentiful supply of trees. The photographer is standing just beyond the terminus in Nether Edge Road, with Sheldon Road on the right and Edwin Smith's chemist's shop on the corner. The tram is one of the balcony cars built around the time of World War One. The blinds for this route were unique in that the 'N' and the 'E' were in red not white, it's thought so as to distinguish them easily from Nether Green. This was the only concession the Corporation made to strangers to the city, because once the early route letters had been dispensed with, the trams carried absolutely no route number, letter or colour to indicate where they were going. The only other major tramway worldwide to do the same was Toronto. The small destination screens did not help either. This short tram route was the second in Sheffield to close, on 24 March 1934. (G. Smith coll.)

The former horse tram depot here functioned as a workshop until at least 1911 and possibly retained some residual functions until 1915, after which it was closed. It is likely that this car, one of the ex-single deck long double deck trams, was turned into an illuminated car at Nether Edge. It was done for the Coronation of King George V and Queen Mary in June 1911. Of the pictures along the top, His Majesty might most have appreciated the warship as he had served in the Royal Navy from the age of twelve and always had something of the look of a naval officer. Almost plastered with light bulbs, the car must have been a fine sight after dark. As an example of the normal standard of workmanship prior to the Second World War, never mind special jobs like this, fully seventeen coats of paint were applied to each car leaving the works. (R.J.S.Wiseman's coll.)

In this Edwardian view Fargate is filled with shoppers, but no traffic except for this one tram. Later, as motor traffic grew, the centre poles had to be removed and then after the trams went the area was pedestrianised. 119, a Brush-built open-top car, runs down the street, then as now a busy part of the city centre. Other areas have tended to go up or down over the years but Fargate has always been fashionable. Route indication went through three stages in the early years; at first names were given on side boards only, then these large route letters were used, and finally route blinds replaced them. Route E for Ecclesall was fine (except at this date it wasn't Ecclesall!), but it was less useful when the trams ran through to the far side of town, as they usually did, in this case either to Osgathorpe (Pitsmoor) or Owlerton. (R.J.S.Wiseman's coll.)

When the tramway in this direction first opened on 13 April 1900 the trams stopped at Hunters Bar but in just over a year were extended to the left towards Nether Green. The Ecclesall service did not start until 1908. The route was shut on 27 March 1954 in the second round of the closure policy agreed by the City Council in 1951. A couple of months beforehand 153 is passing Hunters Bar, probably coming off service as the rear blind still displays Ecclesall when it should have been Middlewood. It is a real winter's day of the kind that seems less and less common now. After the trams ended, the gap in the roundabout was filled in and the gateposts of the old toll bar placed there, much where they were in the days when passing traffic had to pay for the privilege. Don't be misled by what looks like a church spire on the right; it is just a snowy gable end! (R.J.S.Wiseman)

The Ecclesall route was opened on 1 August 1908 and then only to Banner Cross, about half way to the final terminus and where this picture is believed to have been taken. Middlewood via Hillsborough is the correct destination. The conductor posed on the step is Bernard Milner Kitson who later became an inspector and then finally the chief inspector at Pond Street Bus Station. 402 is a Brush rocker panel type, the first fifty of which were delivered like this with single-width destination blinds, later standardised as double. At this period the fleet name and numerals were always painted in this elaborate style and each panel of the bodywork delineated by contrasting gilt lines painted around the edges.

The line reached Ecclesall itself from 14 April 1922, past the parish church and as far as Millhouses Lane. The terminus here had been in the usual position in the centre of the carriageway but when High Storrs School was opened in 1933 there was pressure for a safer alternative. The roadside stop at Woodholm Road was opened in the financial year 1935-1936. Note the trolley reverser in the overhead, a device introduced from 1915 to avoid having to turn the trolley manually using a long bamboo cane. A wartime driver reminisced about trying to tell an elderly man his tram was heading for Ecclesall. 'Tha what?' he said, 'Ecclesall'. Pointing down The Moor he responded, 'Follow tram lines down there and when tha comes to traffic lights turn reight'! (R.J.S.Wiseman)

When the tracks along Pinstone Street required rebuilding in 1909 it was done by laying temporary lines alongside them so that service need not be interrupted. The experience here and in Fitzalan Square makes it plain that the early trackwork was not particularly robust. There was a certain amount of trial and error as electric tramways in the late nineteenth century were an experimental technology. Later both rail and foundations would last longer. It looks as if the centre poles may have been replaced at the same time.

Other tracks relaid during this period were simply closed for the duration. It just shows how little other road traffic there was to consider. By the end of Edward VII's reign most of the trams had received short top covers; one of the 1907 Preston open-balcony cars is visible here. The tram on the left is on the Nether Green route. (R.J.S.Wiseman's coll.)

Around the base of the Crimean column at Moorhead were cannons taken from the battlefield. The Moorish-style glazed shelter was erected as a tramway enquiry office. Note the elaborately dressed lady crossing the road and the gentlemen in their straw boaters; summer or not, though, working men wore caps. This is a splendid picture of one of the original open-top fleet as improved in 1903-5. 133 was built by G.F.Milnes, a firm which over-expanded during the boom years of tramway construction and went into receivership in 1904. However, Milnes Voss, a separate concern formed in 1902 to build tramcar top covers and accessories, provided the covers for sixty-two Sheffield cars like this one. When route blinds began to replace letters this eventually caused the displacement of the headlamp from the upper deck level to the dash. Again the tram is on the Nether Green route.

Moorhead as both a name and place has disappeared from the A-Z Guide for Sheffield. It was the crossroads where Pinstone Street (in the background here) Furnival Street, Backfields and The Moor met. Street furniture includes a splendid gas lamp and the cast iron central standards initially used for the tramway along here. Open-top tram 108 was a Brush 1899 pattern car. This view dates from the early 1900s prior to the changeover from route letters to destination blinds. 108 displays NG for Nether Green, otherwise Fulwood, and indicating a car that has travelled in via Hunters Bar. But can any reader solve the mystery of what the elegant horse-drawn equipage was doing there?

The Nether Green line reached Hangingwater Road from Hunters Bar on 28 October 1901 and Nether Green itself on 14 May 1904. Both it and the alternative route via Broomhill were extended from Nether Green to Fulwood on 12 July 1923. Pictures of the service by tram enthusiasts are rare as the Fulwood terminus was abandoned quite early, on 5 January 1952, as the first stage in the planned conversion of the entire system to buses. Trams reversed on a typical dead-end track in Canterbury Avenue.

SCT Standard 204 looks extremely smart in its impeccably maintained cream livery with the upper deck still in the pre-war style with the Corporation monogram and no advertisements.

A further group of routes left the city via West Street. Standard 210 is about a third of the way on its journey from Crookes to Handsworth on 3 May 1957, the day prior to the closure of the route. This is the Church Street (behind the photographer)/Leopold Street/West Street tramway junction, with the curves from Leopold Street swinging in from the left The smoke-blackened Central Technical School, set up to provide boys with skills required for work in an industrial city, is on the corner. It later became the Education Offices and later still was converted into restaurants and flats. In 1957 Martins Bank (acquired by Barclays in 1969) occupied the corner site in Steel City House between Bow Street (now part of West Street) and Pinfold Street. This is arguably the finest commercial building in Sheffield and was built for HM Office of Works in 1927. Later the civil service reoccupied the ground floor with a Job Centre Plus. (R.J.S.Wiseman)

It is 17 September 1954 and boarding a tram in the middle of the street seems to present no problems to these ladies. The Austin A30 seems to be parked – no double yellow lines then! – and even if it wasn't, the driver would have obeyed the Highway Code and not overtaken the tram on the inside. The A30 had been introduced in 1951 as the 'new Austin 7' and cost just £507. When it went out of production in 1956 nearly 250,000 cars and vans had been sold. Standard 104 is heading for Walkley via West Street and passing the Cavendish Building, built 1910, which then housed the old-established Sheffield Motor Co.; showrooms such as this later all moved further out of town to brownfield sites on the periphery. (R.J.S.Wiseman)

Cars for Crookes plus Fulwood via Broomhill then ran past the University on Western Bank where this car is standing outside the Weston Park gates. The intricate terracotta gate pillars were made by Minton and designed by Godfrey Sykes (1824-1865) of the Sheffield School of Art for the former private owner of the house and park, Thomas Harrison. After 1873 this became Sheffield's first municipal park. The statue just inside the gates is of Ebenezer Elliot, a local poet (1781-1849), most famous for his verses in support of the repeal of the Corn Laws. 255 was one of twelve short top covered cars built new by SCT in 1905, although this carefully posed photograph is dated 1908.

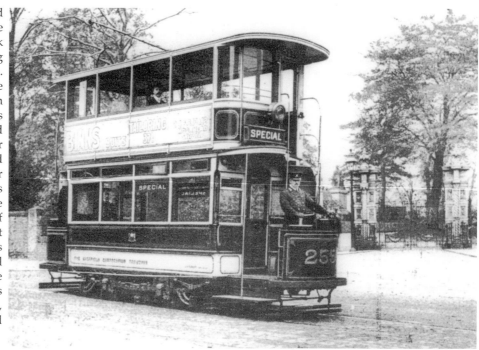

The other line towards Fulwood opened in three fairly swift stages in 1901, first to Manchester Road on 25 March and then by 1 August to Ranmoor Post Office near the point illustrated. Fulwood Road is the expensive end of the city and has scarcely changed in a century. Wood paving, suitably quiet and genteel, was retained here until the 1930s. The type of shop has altered of course. Burgon & Co was a grocer's; they are advertising tea in their window. The nearer shop belonged to Fred Oates & Sons and was offering pickled ox tongues. The inhabitants of the suburb would have been early motor car users, which probably accounts for the pre-war closure of this route in 1936. By 12 October 1901 trams were running to Storth Lane, Nether Green, not quite Fulwood but always so described when travelling via Broomhill. The terminus was on a very steep hill and, as a safety measure, a short extension was added in 1909 to take it over the summit. Route NG reached to the same place via Hunters Bar on 14 May 1904 and was nearer the truth in describing the terminus as Nether Green.

This is a very early view before the introduction of route letters and when the only destination indication was given by a side-mounted board. 107 is a Brush car, with the curtains still in place within the saloon. This route, like the other one, was extended to Fulwood in 1923. (Commercial postcard (picturesheffield.com))

This curve from Crookes Road into Whitham Road was still described as Crookes Junction, even after the Fulwood line had closed on 22 August 1936. Broomhill is a popular residential area and a lot of students now live there, so it still has quite a lively little shopping centre. Snow didn't stay white long on a busy street in an industrial city! Car 53 is on a peak hour service to Brightside via Savile Street. (R.J.S.Wiseman)

In 1901 the Crookes terminus was at Lydgate Lane, not far up from Broomhill. On 28 April 1902 the tracks reached School Road, so-called because of St. Thomas's School, out of sight to the left here, and dating from 1791. Perhaps the girls in their white Edwardian dresses and blouses were pupils there? The print has been dated 1900, but destination indicators were not introduced until later in that decade. The indicator still also has space for a route letter; maybe the initial plan was to use both?

In 1920-21 a new tram shed was built on Pickmere Road and a junction was laid in for access across the end of School Road, just on the right in the previous view. The building with its alternating bands of brick and stone was an elegant one and it was the highest tram depot in the country. After its closure on 1 June 1957 (or 4 May, sources differ) it was used for a while by other council departments and then demolished. The St. Vincent's Church complex occupies the site now. 130 was an SCT Standard and it is coming back on shed after carrying out a short working to Darnall.

The trams were extended to Heavygate Road just before the First War on 26 November 1913. This then became the highest terminus in Sheffield and one of the highest in the country. The actual summit of the system was a few hundred yards towards the city along Northfield Road where the tracks rose to 729 ft (222 m) above sea level. Even despite this, every effort was made to keep the trams running during the winter. The bombing on 12 December 1940 had virtually destroyed fourteen trams. Even under wartime conditions Queens Road managed to replace them all between 1941and 1944 with new ones (reusing their old numbers) to the 1936 design. 430 entered service on 3 July 1944. (R.J.S.Wiseman)

The first section of the Walkley branch was very pleasant along Crookes Valley Road. This is on an embankment above the valley and on one side is a small park with a lake, on the other a recreation ground. Little has changed. Standard 62 is outbound. (R.J.S.Wiseman)

Barber Road comes next, quite a stiff climb for the trams. The double line almost fills the road as two cars pass numbers 16 and 18, both still shops today. In May 1955 the track was being repaired but less than a year later, on 7 April 1956, the Walkley route was closed. Presumably there was a safety critical fault that had to be attended to. 74, going to Intake, was involved in the post-war programme to rehabilitate as many of the Standard class as was possible and had received new upholstery in both saloons in March 1951. It is not, incidentally, the 74 which is preserved as older numbers vacated by a sale, as in this case, or by scrapping were often reused. (R.J.S.Wiseman)

Delivery of the first trams, both double and single deck, lasted over 1899-1904. Sixty-nine were single deckers. Most of the latter later had their platforms extended and nine had them enclosed; twenty-one were rebuilt as double deckers, thirty-five were sold and nine were converted to snowploughs, the last single deck passenger services being withdrawn in 1921. This is Springvale on the Walkley route, which was very hilly, meaning that the Board of Trade originally demanded the use of single deck trams, as they did to Intake (which is what the 'I' stood for).

South Road was the second highest terminus after Crookes. The line to Walkley was only about two miles long and was opened in one fell swoop on 18 September 1899, only the second route after Tinsley – Nether Edge and, given the severe gradients, quite an achievement. The road seems to fall over a cliff at the end of the street, giving some idea of how steep the hills are in this part of the city. The only town whose trams really beat Sheffield's in this respect was Halifax. The shop behind the tram was a baker's which proudly advertised pikelets (crumpets to southerners). There were two routes from Walkley, one to the LMS Station – Standard 114 is going there – and the other to Intake.

Angel Street and Snig Hill in the city are virtually indistinguishable. First of all a dead-end siding was built in the former and only in 1904 were the tracks extended down into Snig Hill to make a through line. It was used inter alia by Ecclesall – Middlewood cars. The flats and shops in Corporation Buildings on the right were built about 1905. These looked somewhat run-down a century later but work has recently been completed to refurbish what remains of the block. The diversion provided a junction with Bridge Street and after 1928 to the Tenter Street Depot. As part of the run-down of the system the line was made into single track in 1955 as by then it was normally used only in the downhill direction to reach the depot. On March 27 the same year one of the last enthusiasts' tours of what remained of the system took place. When 222 entered the depot at Tinsley at 3.34 p.m. on 8 October 1960, it became the very last Corporation tram in passenger service. It was Richard Wiseman (photographer of many of the images in this book) who persuaded the depot foreman to use this particular car! (A.D.Packer)

Standard 29, turning from Fargate into High Street, will be using Angel Street to reach Holme Lane Depot at Malin Bridge. The passenger service had already been withdrawn but the depot was still in use. The Telegraph building, at that time still the 'front of office' premises for both the Sheffield Telegraph and the evening paper, The Star, is in the background. The press now occupy buildings further back and Telegraph House itself is a bank. The crowds are there for a visit by Princess Margaret, on 18 April 1953. Remarkably this did not call for the suspension of tram services. (R.J.S.Wiseman)

No pictures of a salt car or a new works car have come to light. However, 349 is a stores car and was formerly Preston passenger tram 271/349 until 1951. Here it is entering Tenter Street Depot, officially opened on 20 September and in use between 23 October 1928 and 8 October 1960. The car looks as if it is painted in blue and cream rather than the more usual grey for works vehicles. For many years these UEC-built trams were exceptional in the Sheffield fleet because their windscreens were far enough from the controls not to require the otherwise almost universal 'banjo' glasses (so-called because they were shaped like that once-popular instrument). 349 was decorated with coloured lights as an illuminated tram for the closing procession on 8 October 1960. It then went to Crich where it was used to house a generator for some years until eventually being scrapped. Tenter Street was built on a hillside and was a two-storey building with trams below and buses above. (R.J.S.Wiseman)

The Corporation route to Middlewood and Malin Bridge used almost exactly the same roads as Supertram does today. That does not apply to the route taken out of the city, however, as Supertram leaves along West Street. Anyone who knows the British summer will recognise when this picture was taken! This is the City Hall stop, the next one out from Cathedral, in 1995. Leopold Street is out of sight to the right and Steel City House is on the left beside car 08. After Supertram opened to Fitzalan Square in March 1994 work was concentrated elsewhere and trams did not reach Cathedral until 18 February 1995 and then Shalesmoor on the 27th. The tram is in the grey livery and the blind still reads only South Yorkshire Supertram with destinations proper left to a board in the cab window. Drivers often forgot to change the board and this car is actually not going to Shalesmoor but returning from there.

The 'old' trams reached Infirmary Road via West Bar. Supertram turns right at the top of West Street onto the median strip of the inner ring road at the University stop just prior to Brook Hill. This is a critical road junction where the ring road, Brook Hill (up to the university) and a connection from the city centre meet at a busy roundabout. Few drivers can miss it for long! Supertram avoids the problem by diving underneath. In light rail parlance this is an underpass and not a tunnel, the latter being reserved for sections which include an underground station.

In May 1994 work had only just begun on the new Supertram line along Infirmary Road and the whole area was in a state of flux. This photograph was taken from the Kelvin flats, system-built concrete low rise blocks put up in the 1960s. Traffic projections for Supertram took their inhabitants into account but by the time the trams were running the unloved buildings had been demolished, eventually to be replaced by some quite nice mixed housing. The older properties, on the far side of the street, however, are still standing.

What were officially classed as Improved Standard trams were known universally as domed-roof cars. Like most of the previous Standards they were home-built and the result was a much more 'Thirties' appearance with curves instead of angles. Much effort was expended on providing opening upper deck windows and several designs were fitted, though none proved entirely satisfactory in service. The other obvious external difference was the panelling across the lower saloon ventilation windows, which had air scoops inserted for ventilation either side of the

side destination screen. Mechanically the cars were identical to the straight-sided Standards. 231-242 & 249-303 were made in 1936-1939 and ran until they were withdrawn between 1957 and 1960. 233 is shown here on 7 June 1938 in Infirmary Road and demonstrates how smart these trams looked before the war. Their overall cream livery was continued on to the roof and this, together with the municipal crest and the transport department's monogram proudly displayed on the sides, gave the trams a particularly smart appearance. (H.B.Priestley/NTM)

The Malin Bridge spur has always been the terminus of a cross-city route, from Fulwood in Corporation days and nowadays from Halfway. The junction at Hillsborough Corner requires restrictions on other traffic to make it workable for Supertram, a feature not always popular with motorists. Here a tram is turning out of Langsett Road into Holme Lane. The interlaced track here is a device to pre-sort trams at junctions which has been used on tramways for many years. 116 has an advertising livery for the Meadowhall Shopping Centre. There is always at least one car 'painted' overall like this for Meadowhall and usually at least one other turned out for a different advertiser.

Hillsborough was the destination for the third horse tram service which was opened on 19 May 1877. This is Holme Lane Depot. One of double deck series 22-31. provided by Starbuck, is on the left. The car on the right is one of twelve Milnes open-sided cars bought by the Corporation in 1897, very late in the horse tram era. They might have been ideal for a seaside resort like Douglas, Isle of Man, where similar cars are still used, but they were highly unpopular in wet and snowy Sheffield conditions and saw little use. The depot staff are posed with the tools of their trades, a smith with a horseshoe, the grooms with brushes. A goat was often kept at the stables because it was thought that in case of fire it would keep calm and lead the more excitable horses to safety. The Hillsborough horse cars were withdrawn in 1902 prior to the electrification of the system.

The horse tram depot was not reused at once but the growing fleet caused it to be reconstructed in 1914. The electric branch had been opened on 19 May 1908. During the 1914-1918 war women were employed as conductresses for the first time. One, after arguing with a passenger, remarked, 'How I would like to make him suffer!' to which a voice replied 'Marry 'im Miss'! Female staff were essential again in World War Two. The shed finally closed on 30 April 1954 – about two years after the branch had lost its passenger service – and Richard Wiseman took this atmospheric shot inside a

month earlier. Electric tram depots were dangerous places for the unwary, with maintenance pits along the length of most tracks and high gantries for cleaning the upper decks of the trams. 366 was the 1918 experimental car which was the precursor for all the later rocker panel trams; it was withdrawn and scrapped on or just before the closure of the depot. (R.J.S.Wiseman)

Surprisingly the entrance doorways to the old depot are still standing to this day. The whole area behind them was cleared a number of years ago and used for a new medical centre, but the front wall was retained and emblazoned with the title 'Tramways Medical Centre'. The sharp-eyed might spot that Supertram even has a span wire attached to the wall, maintaining its tramway function. 118 is outward bound on the Blue route to Halfway. The width of the road means that there is no room for a stop along here, even had one been thought necessary. About half the system is on streets like this, and the remainder is either ballasted railway track or on viaducts or bridges. Operation is on line of sight, but road junctions and key locations, such as the Meadowhall single line, require signals.

105 is just moving off the double line into the single track off-street terminal at the end of the spur. The road on the left is Ball Street and this is still very much an area of traditional terraced housing. The Corporation trams travelled a couple of hundred yards further down Holme Lane before reaching their on-street terminus. The Malin Bridge – Halfway line is the Blue route, shown by the square on the destination display. In 1995 an Orange service was operated on Sundays from Malin Bridge to Herdings Park and there was also a Purple route from Halfway direct to Meadowhall, bypassing the city centre. On weekdays in 1995 Green trams ran from Herdings to city only. The car here is in the latest livery, launched on 21 January 2006 with number 115. The design brief was handled by Atkins Rail, but the painting was all done 'in-house'. Stagecoach had decided to overhaul the cars twice in their planned lifespan instead of only once.

Two cars are queuing at the old terminus. The factory chimney, no longer there, belonged to Burgon & Ball & Co. Ltd. The firm itself, established in 1830. is still on site and is arguably the most fascinating survivor of Sheffield's light trades. On 11 March 1864 much of Malin Bridge was destroyed in the flood caused after the Dale Dyke Dam burst its banks and in 1873 the firm built the La Plata Works on land made available as a result. Famous for manufacturing sheep shears, the firm has diversified into garden tools today. It even had a go at manufacturing La Plata motor cars early in the twentieth century. Malin Bridge to Fulwood was the first casualty of the closure report on 5 January 1952 making this a particularly interesting view.

A couple of hundred yards further on along the 'main line' to Middlewood, 121 is passing Hillsborough Park. The Adam-style hall in the background was built in 1779 for a Mr Thomas Stead who named it in honour of Viscount Downe of Hillsborough, County Down; later the Hillsborough name was transferred to the suburb. The hall was home after that to three Sheffield industrialists, in turn a cutler, a locomotive designer and a silversmith. It was gifted to the city in 1906 and is now a rather grand branch library. The tram is in the post-2006 paint scheme. For safety reasons the doors have to be highlighted in yellow.

Standard 178 is reversing here at Carlton Road crossover, a little way in towards town and almost exactly where the modern Leppings Lane stop is on Supertram. It was quite near the Parkside Road link used on match days. Incidentally Parkside Road was the furthest that tracks reached when the line was opened on 30 May 1903.

The crowds at the Wednesday football ground on Penistone Road required so large a fleet of trams to transport them that Parkside Road was not long enough to contain them all. Other cars were stacked at Middlewood terminus while the match was being played. To permit service cars to reverse, and to manoeuvre the specials, three extra crossovers were laid in between Parkside Road and the terminus. This is the scene on 20 February 1954, before extensive route closures caused some supporters to travel by bus rather than tram. The first car is a Cravens rocker panel type 494. This series was the last to be built new with wooden seats. The route down here had been extended from Parkside Road to Catch Bar Lane on 8 September 1913 and then to the final terminus on 26 November. It was closed on 27 March 1954. (R.J.S.Wiseman)

The Supertram terminus is a stub track on one side of the road next to the Park & Ride car park in the background. At 2007 rates motorists using the tram could leave their cars here for less than £1, a lot less than paying for parking in the city centre. An extra 150 spaces were added in October 2007 so using the tram is clearly becoming more popular. Supertram also started a bus link to Stocksbridge in 2007 which runs from the car park every ten minutes Monday to Saturday, at the same frequency as the tram. This innovative approach won a top award at the 2007 Light Rail Conference organised by the LRTA. The Middlewood line opened in two stages, to Shalesmoor on 27 February and throughout on 23 October 1995.

To trace the Wadsley Bridge route it is necessary to revisit the city centre one last time. The original stone arches of Lady's Bridge, named after the chapel to the Blessed Virgin erected at the southern end, date from 1486 to 1487. Though rebuilt several times, it must be one of the few medieval structures in the city still serving its purpose. All bridges above here were swept away in the 1864 flood after the Dale Dyke disaster. 472 is outbound to Brightside via Savile Street. 296 is a Hillsborough football special and once across the river it will be turning right into Bridge Street. The junction on the left here leads into Nursery Street. In 1954 most products were British-made by long-established firms and that included Raleigh bicycles. The 'tram jam' is on Lady's Bridge with 296 now entering Bridge Street with a full load of supporters going to the Sheffield Wednesday (or 'Owls') ground at Hillsborough. 447 is going in to pick up more fans. An inspector is on duty to direct traffic. The lines along Bridge Street were laid at the same time as those in Snig Hill and were not used by any of the regular services, but they did provide a convenient way of moving trams to the football ground without having to bring them through the city centre. The building to the left of Castlegate (which never had tracks down it) was built in the mid-1900s as a four storey stable for the Midland Railway's dray horses. It later became a warehouse and later still was converted into flats. 447 was a Brush rocker panel car put into service in July 1920 and still with three years to run after this picture was taken on March 20 1954. (Both R.J.S.Wiseman)

In 1942 ten 1920-21 English Electric open-balcony trams were purchased from Bradford, converted from their 4'0" gauge, renumbered 325-334, fully enclosed, and given a plain grey wartime livery. They had similar trucks to the ex-Newcastle cars but D.K. 31D motors and DB1 Form K4 controllers. Of the fifty-nine seats, most were upstairs. 333, ex-Bradford 219, is just passing the junction for West Bar Green and Tenter Street Depot. This area has totally changed as nearly all the property has been demolished to make way for a new roundabout associated with the recent extension of the inner ring road. The buildings in the far distance at the bottom of Snig Hill provide a reference. The Bradford trams were not popular with crews who regarded them as much inferior to home-built cars, but the purchase was necessary to help cope with heavy wartime traffic to the steel factories. All the class was withdrawn in 1950-1951 at the same as the new Roberts cars were being delivered. 330's lower deck was re-used for the system's water/track grinding car. The flags were out on the same corner on 27 October 1954 for a visit by the Queen and Prince Philip. The very distinctive building in the background was built in 1914 and has been variously known as The Hostel, Tudor House and the Mayfair Flats. The corner block was demolished in connection with the road works mentioned above. 451 is a Cravens rocker panel and is running off-shed from Tenter Street and turning out from West Bar Green into West Bar towards Middlewood. It may well be a football special going to pick up returning supporters. (2nd pic. R.J.S Wiseman)

The Wadsley Bridge route seemed always to have a good proportion of streamliners. There were a couple of lengths of single line in Neepsend which were never doubled. The original parliamentary powers had said that the track was not to be closer to the kerbs than 9ft 6in if one third of the frontagers objected and this, together with the problem of getting street-widening powers, meant that much of the early system used single and loop construction. 536 is about to regain double track at Mowbray Street.

There is still a surprising amount of small scale industry in the area today, although some of the premises to the left along the river bank have been replaced by modern flats in recent years. 536 was the very last tram added to the Corporation fleet, on 11 April 1952. Apart from the Blackpool Coronation and Centenary cars plus a false start in Leeds, the Roberts cars were the final new tram design in England until the era of modern light rail; they were certainly the swansong of the 2-axle truck. (R.J.S.Wiseman)

Standard 87, reconstructed after the war, joins Penistone Road at Hillfoot Bridge on 30 September 1959. Just three days later this tram service was turned over to buses. Trams first reached here via Nursery Street on 26 January 1901. The direct tracks along the main road were added on 12 February 1903, but were only used for special workings such as to the Owls ground at Hillsborough. The enormous gasometers at Neepsend exploded at 11.35 p.m. on 12 December 1940 after being bombed, part of a very frightening night. This is 30 September 1959 and just three days later this tram service was turned over to buses.

Virtually all Sheffield trams had bodies constructed in the traditional manner on wooden frames. In 1931 an interesting experiment involved building a body in rigid metal using 'Duralumin', an aluminium alloy including a small proportion of copper. That made it lighter than similar cars and so 370 had less powerful MV 116Z 40HP motors with obvious advantages in power consumption. However, the higher initial outlay was possibly the reason why this remained a one-off. According to one source 370 ended up with 50HP motors, which was highly possible for reasons of standardisation, and was scrapped in May 1957. The first picture shows it in the queue of football cars in Parkside Road and the end-on view demonstrates the wider than average window struts, necessary to ensure the body's rigidity. Then 370 is seen again on Penistone Road North near Herries Road South, Owlerton. Trams did not start running along here out to Wadsley Bridge itself until 7 June 1924. Today this is one of the busiest dual carriageways in the city and it is regularly nose-to-tail with motor traffic at peak periods. The split between the left and the right hand sides has not changed – a long line of terraces on the one side and somewhat down-at-heel commercial premises on the other. (1st pic. R.J.S.Wiseman)

Four trams were built by SCT as prototypes between 1918 and 1921. 366 seated seventy-six on benches downstairs and transverse reversible seats upstairs, except for the bays, where there were facing benches for four passengers per side. It had a Peckham P22 8'6" (2591 mm) truck (universal for new cars until 1946), BTH RHE 203 40HP motors and BTH controllers. The other three cars seem to have been almost the same and all prefigured the later rocker panels. 367 entered service on 7 March 1919 and last received a medium overhaul in 1949 when, in common with four other cars, it received a more modern platforms without banjo glasses. It is pictured in the line-up of football specials on Parkside Road on 20 March 1954 just about to pass a couple of Inspectors. The regular service only ran as far as Parkside Road until 1924, when it was extended to Wadsley Bridge. (R.J.S.Wiseman)

Standard 85 is descending Halifax Road just north of the railway bridge at Wadsley Bridge. At the time the photographer could stand on the station platform here, but that and all passenger services are long gone with now only a single line for heavy freight traffic to the Stocksbridge steelworks. The little shop is on the corner of Fox Hill Road. Park Drive cigarettes are still available today, but advertisements like this are a thing of the past. The old buildings across the street were later demolished and have been replaced by a retail park. The terminus was half a mile or so up the hill, some distance short of the massive pre-war housing estate at Parson Cross. The fact that trams didn't serve the expanding rim of the city was of course one reason why the more flexible bus was chosen in 1951. In contrast, the Supertram lines run right out to modern developments such as Halfway and Meadowhall. (R.J.S.Wiseman)

The Last Tram Procession took place on 8 October 1960. Fifteen trams were involved, travelling out from Tenter Street to Beauchief and back to either Tinsley or Queens Road. Clifford Gallimore was an assistant wireman and remembered following the last car of all through to Tinsley. 'As the tram passed the various section breakers we cut off the power for the last time, prior to dismantling all the overhead wire and fittings. On the last night people kept putting pennies on the track for souvenirs'. Before the regular service ceased at 3.30 p.m. streamliner 519 is passing the depot on its way to Vulcan Road. At this stage there is no sign of it being an occasion and the tram is nearly empty. The drivers of the cars tailing the tram, however, are probably thinking 'Thank goodness! I shan't be doing this tomorrow'. Not surprisingly cleaning standards had slipped and 519 looks quite dingy. Selected cars had been cleaned up and a few repainted for the final procession but normal service was left to workaday fleet.

Also on the Last Day, two of the cars operating the passenger service stop on the loading bay in Pinstone Street outside the town hall. 102 was one of the few remaining Standard trams and 501 behind was the prototype for the Roberts cars. Rather ironically, given the abortive experiment in the 1930s with one-way traffic along here, buses today are one-way along here. The modern scene has been opened out with the removal of the passenger shelters and, more recently, with the redevelopment of the Peace Gardens. But that apart this remains a quintessential Sheffield scene dominated, as it has been for 110 years, by the fine Victorian town hall.

Forty-seven years later, however, Supertram belies the pessimism of the 1950s or, more properly, the idealistic idea that motorbuses were the solution to the woes of public transport. Between 1978 and the end of 2007 there have been 125 new tramway or light rail systems worldwide, together with 44 heritage tramways which provide at least a limited public service. The change has been quite dramatic, though sadly far less so in the UK than elsewhere in the world. Sheffield was fortunate to obtain grant aid to build its new system. Car 120 is at Hollinsend Road on the outer ring road between Manor Top and Gleadless and is running on a service between Hendings Park and Meadowhall. The flats behind it belong to the Graves Trust, one of the many benefactions of Alderman J. G. Graves who also gave his name to the extensive park near the former Meadowhead tram terminus. Past and present meet in a city where the public good has always been a matter of concern to its citizens and to its political leaders.

Appendix

HORSE TRAMS

Company Horse Trams

The Sheffield Tramways Co. owned a total of 53 trams during its lifetime, but never more than 50 at any one time. The majority were double deck, nos. 1-12 and 22-31 being built in two batches in 1873 and 1877 by the Starbuck Car & Wagon Co. of Birkenhead, the earliest firm to enter the business on any scale. 32-40 were added in 1877 but their builder is unknown. 1 (a replacement) and 50 were delivered by the Ashbury Co. of Manchester in 1886. These were of a type known as the Eades reversible whereby the entire body could be swivelled on the truck at a terminus to avoid having to unhitch the horses. A similar car has recently been restored and can be seen at the Heaton Park museum tramway in Manchester. Replacement car 12 and another (number unknown) arrived in 1887 and they were the only ones in the fleet to have forward-facing 'garden' seats instead of the old-fashioned longitudinal knifeboard seat on the top deck.Starbucks had also delivered single deck trams 13-20 in 1874, nos. 21 and 41-45 were added in 1877 and finally 46-49 in 1884, all by unknown builders. Five single-deckers were later converted to double deck. Most trams needed two horses, but some light single-deckers required only one. Preserved car 15 was of this type.

Corporation Horse Trams

In order to operate new routes, the Corporation bought twelve double-deckers of varying capacity and the same number of single deck covered 'toastrack' cars from G. F. Milnes, who had taken over Starbuck's works, in 1897/8. The latter type resembled the breakfast table item by having rows of seats across the full width of the body and were open-sided; hardly practical in the Sheffield climate! Some replaced Company trams but 51-67 were additional to the fleet. Twelve horse trams were converted for electric operation, all but two as works cars.

ELECTRIC TRAMS BY TYPE

[1] Double deck '1899' pattern

In 1899-1904 Sheffield Corporation equipped its new tramway with 245 trams. The greater number were open top double deck cars and most of them had this equipment – Brill 21E 6'0" (1829 mm) trucks (but see notes below), General Electric Co., Witton, Birmingham GE52 25HP motors (GE58 35HP from 131) and British-Thomson-Houston, Rugby, B13 controllers. Several car builders were involved – Milnes 1-38 (Cantilever trucks, Peckham Truck & Engineering Co,

Kingston, NY – like Brill licensed in UK), 131-155; Electric Railway & Tramway Carriage Works Ltd (ER&TC Co.), Preston, 59-88; Brush 104-123, 219-243 (and Brush trucks); Cravens Railway Carriage & Wagon Co Ltd, Darnall, Sheffield 167-186; Sheffield Corporation Tramways (SCT, at Netheredge Works) 193-198, 213-218 (Milnes Girder trucks), 244/245 (rebuilt horse cars, Brush trucks). All of them later received varying types of top cover.

[2] Single deck '1899' pattern

There were sixty nine single deck passenger trams built in the same period, mostly having BTH GE52 motors until re-equipped with GE58. BTH B13 controllers were used plus Brill 21E 6'0" (1829 mm) trucks. Builders were as follows – Milnes 39-52 (Peckham Cantilever 10A trucks), 187-192; ER&TC Co. 53-58; Brush 89-103; SCT 124-129, 200-211; Cravens 156-165. There were wooden longitudinal seats except for 51, 52 and 56 which were (or became) non-standard. There were also four works trams, two of the latter being converted horse cars. Some passenger cars were later converted to works vehicles and others into large double deck trams. More were sold and the last ran in 1921.

[3] Short canopy double deck

The Corporation built twelve of this design in 1905 and converted many more of the earlier type. Preserved car 74 is an example.

[4] 'Preston' cars

Nos. 258-272 were built by the United Electric Car Co. (UEC, successor to the ER&TC Co.) in 1907 and were the first to have enclosed drivers' platforms from new. They initially used Mountain & Gibson radial trucks, an unsatisfactory design, which were replaced by the more robust Peckham P.22 type, these having 8'0" (2438 mm) wheelbases. The usual GE motors were replaced in 1926 by the BTH type RGE20 (except 260 & 268, Metropolitan Vickers 102, & 272, BTH 503) and the BTH B.13 controllers by BTH B510. There were longitudinal wooden seats below and transverse above for 58 passengers. The class was fully enclosed in 1924-27, including 259 which had been experimentally converted in 1911 and 263 and 269 which had balcony screens fitted for a while. Seating was increased to 62. All were renumbered 336-350 in 1937. Four were withdrawn from passenger service before World War II and the remainder by 1947-54. 346 became a driver training tram and two others were cut down as works cars.

[5] Open ended

The Tramways department built nos. 281-295 at their new

Queens Road Works in 1912 with a full length top cover but retaining open platforms and balconies. They had Brill 21E trucks, GE203 40HP motors and BTH B18 controllers. 290 was fully enclosed following an accident in 1919. Forty four of type [3] were converted to the same design in 1911-13. and of these 235 and 243 were further rebuilt with enclosed top decks in 1924-5. Whereas 6, though at first turned out as a vestibuled car in 1913, was rebuilt to open-platform configuration in 1920. Withdrawal of these cars was completed over the decade 1923-33.

[6] Open balcony

Nos. 296-355 were built with enclosed drivers' platforms but open bays above in 1913-15 by Brush and the Corporation. They had Brill 21E trucks, BTH RGE20 or BTH GE203 40HP motors and the usual controllers. Sixteen older cars were converted to this style.

[7] ex-LCC B class

To meet a wartime shortage of trams, twenty six of these London County Council trams were transferred to South Yorkshire in 1917-18, six being used in Rotherham until transferred to Sheffield in 1926. Unlike other Sheffield trams of the period, they had open platforms but fully enclosed upper decks. Trucks were Brill 21E or Peckham P22 of 6'6" (1981 mm) or 7'0" (2134 mm) and controllers Dick Kerr DB1 Form D or BTH. Motors were DK 25A, BTH GE58 or BTH 203. There were 56 seats, including longitudinal plywood ones in the lower saloon. They were not used for long and the last were withdrawn in 1931.

[8] Enclosed rebuilds

Seventy five trams, including two 'Prestons', were rebuilt with fully enclosed platforms and upper decks in the period 1919-1925 and almost all had been withdrawn by 1939. The enclosed balconies were rather amateur affairs. The full series of 1919-25 comprised 177, 179, 194, 197, 214, 220, 224, 229, 230, 234-7, 239, 243, 290, 296-349. 351, 354 &355 (plus Prestons 263 and 269). Trucks were Brill 21E (except 349 Peckham P22 and 355 Brill Radiax 9'0" or 2743 mm), controllers standard B18s and motors BTH GE203 40HP. The 62 seats were mostly longitudinal except in the upper deck saloon. The top decks had sliding door bulkheads.

[9] Rocker panel Standards

If the four experimental trams constructed at Queens Road are included, there were 154 of these cars. The production series was built by Brush (36-50, 376-450, respectively in 1919-22 and 1924-25) and Cravens (451-500 in 1926-27). They had Peckham P22 8'6" trucks (2591 mm) and BTH controllers; those on 451-500 were the BTH OK1B type. Most motors were BTH GE203 40HP except for 36-60 (BTH B503) and 451-500 (MV102D 50HP). Like prototype 366, the first series had seventy-six seats but this was later reduced to sixty-eight by having 2/1 instead of 2/2 seating upstairs to assist the conductors passing down the cars. Side benches were used downstairs. The last two series had air brakes fitted and these were retrofitted to the earlier ones, including 366-369. Most cars were later upholstered throughout. Two were lost by enemy action and 493 was withdrawn after an accident in 1946, the remainder followed in 1950-57.

[10] Straight-sided Standard

This class was even larger at 210 (212 if experimental cars 1 and 370 are included) and was produced in the period 1928-36, mostly at Queens Road but with a few cars built by W. & E. Hill Ltd. A handful were in service until the end, in 1960. Mechanically and electrically they were very similar to 451-500. From 1952 to 1956 the lower decks of twenty three cars were completely taken apart and reconstructed at Queens Road. This involved numbers 25, 27, 68, 69, 72, 75, 87, 89, 97, 98, 102, 115, 122, 128, 151, 161, 167, 170, 173, 174, 183 and 191. The saloons of all but car 87 were rebuilt in the style of the domed-roof trams except that air scoops were not fitted. Various other cars were overhauled and improved. Maintenance standards were always high in Sheffield.

[11] Domed roof

This improved version of the Standard tram was again built locally and was put into service between 1936 and the outbreak of war in 1939. Except for the bodywork they were identical to the previous class. Two together with a dozen older trams were destroyed by air raids and all were replaced by new ones to the latest design in 1941-1944, most using the original truck. These comprised two rocker panel (430 & 483), ten Standard (83, 85, 100, 112, 119, 129, 133, 192, 201 & 227) and two domed-roof (261 & 264) cars.

[12] Ex-Newcastle

311-314 were purchased from Newcastle Corporation in 1941 and rebuilt for further service in Sheffield. They had had Brill 21E trucks, GE58 35HP motors and BTH B3 or B18 controllers.

[13] Ex-Bradford

These old trams, built in 1920-21 by English Electric (the successor to UEC), had Brill 21E trucks and Dick Kerr equipment. They were acquired and rebuilt for Sheffield in 1943 but all had been withdrawn by 1951.

[14] Roberts cars

The last Corporation-built tram was streamliner 501, followed in 1950-52 by 502-36 from Roberts of Horbury, Wakefield. All had Maley & Taunton hornless type 588 trucks with the exceptional wheelbase of 9'0" (2743 mm), Metropolitan Vickers 101 DR3 65HP motors and BTH N510 controllers. There were 62 upholstered seats. 502-536 had all-metal bodies rather than wood-framed. The last few arrived after the decision to abandon the tramway system had been taken.

[15] Preserved trams

In approximate date order the trams which survived the abandonment were horse car 15, single decker 46, early double decker 74 (not directly but via Gateshead), stores car 349 (later scrapped), Preston car 264, works car (ex-Bradford) 330, Standard 189, domed-roof 264, and Roberts cars 510 and 513. The South Yorkshire Transport Museum, which was housed until recently in Tinsley Depot and now at Waddington Way in Rotherham, possesses the lower deck of rocker panel car 460. Some of these cars are illustrated in the body of the book